KEY

JURISPRUDENCE

PETER HALSTEAD

Hodder Arnold

A MEMBER OF THE HODDER HEA

Orders: please contact Bookpoint Ltd, 130 Milton Park, Abingdon, Oxon OX14 4SB.
Telephone: (44) 01235 827720. Fax: (44) 01235 400454. Lines are open from 9.00–6.00,
Monday to Saturday, with a 24-hour message answering service.
Email address: orders@bookpoint.co.uk

British Library Cataloguing in Publication Data
A catalogue record for this title is available from The British Library.

ISBN-10: 0 340 88695 1
ISBN-13: 978 0 340 88695 3

This edition published 2005
Impression number   10 9 8 7 6 5 4 3 2 1
Year   2010 2009 2008 2007 2006 2005

Hodder Headline's policy is to use papers that are natural, renewable and recyclable products
and made from wood grown in sustainable forests. The logging and manufacturing processes
are expected to conform to the environmental regulations of the country of origin.

Typeset by Transet Limited, Coventry, England.
Printed in Great Britain for Hodder Arnold, an imprint of Hodder Education, a member of
the Hodder Headline Group, 338 Euston Road, London NW1 3BH by Cox & Wyman Ltd,
Reading, Berkshire.

CONTENTS

Preface

The Key Facts series is designed to give a clear view of each subject.
This will be useful to students when tackling new topics and is
invaluable as a revision aid. Most chapters open with an outline in
diagram form of the points covered in that chapter. The points are
then developed in list form to make learning easier. Traditional
'black letter' law subjects provide supporting cases but students may
be pleased to learn that this is only occasionally appropriate for
legal theory.

The topics covered in this Key Facts Jurisprudence range from
Greek, Roman and Christian ideas through the philosophers of the
Enlightenment and Reformation eras and into modern times, tracing
the development of natural law theory to its current human rights
provenance, the rise of legal positivism, and the many and varied
alternative and complementary methodologies and creeds that now
span the field.

Because of this wide range of materials, the compact format of the
book, and the fact that jurisprudence is taught at different levels, all
students coming to the subject for the first time should find it useful
for both initial study and revision purposes.

The law is stated as I believe it to be on 1st June 2005.

Peter Halstead

CHAPTER 1

JURISPRUDENCE

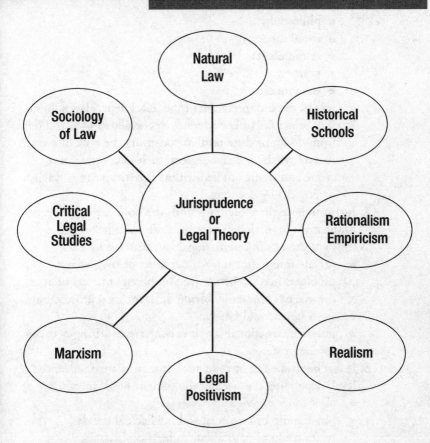

- Natural Law
- Historical Schools
- Rationalism Empiricism
- Realism
- Legal Positivism
- Marxism
- Critical Legal Studies
- Sociology of Law

Jurisprudence or Legal Theory

1.1 OVERVIEW

1.1.1 Reasons for study

1. The main purpose of studying jurisprudence or legal theory is to provide a framework within which students can locate and reflect upon all aspects of their study of law, including its:

- origins, history and development;
- intellectual foundations and justifications;
- relationship to other academic and practical disciplines, such as:
  - philosophy;
  - social theory;
  - criminology;
  - politics;
  - economics;
- role in the interpretation of the 'black letter' law subjects (i.e. principles of law which are generally known and free from doubt or dispute) that constitute the bulk of most A-level syllabi and law degrees, such as contract, tort, crime and so on, studied within a particular (e.g. English or French) legal system.

2. Jurisprudence therefore transcends the boundaries between municipal (i.e. national) laws, yet still needs to be distinguished from international law, which may be:
   - private international law, or conflict of laws, where problems need to be resolved on private matters such as divorce or contract involving different legal jurisdictions, e.g. England and Ghana;
   - public international law, involving issues arising between sovereign states.

3. It can be studied at introductory, intermediate or advanced level, depending on whether the student needs to gain a:
   - clear bird's eye view;
   - broad grasp of historical and intellectual trends (e.g. the relationship of natural law to legal positivism);
   - more detailed grasp of particular concepts (e.g. realism, sociology of law, rights or economic law calculus, or the idea of justice).

For all levels this book provides a useful reference and revision tool.

4. This first chapter outlines many of the concepts and ideas that constitute legal theory, which are amplified and explained further in subsequent chapters.

1.1.2 Meaning of 'jurisprudence'

1. The word 'jurisprudence' is derived from the Latin *juris prudentia*, generally meaning knowledge or study of the (social) science of law, although it may mean other things in particular contexts, e.g.:
   - case law;
   - laws of a particular jurisdiction, e.g. French law;
   - particular 'families' of law, e.g. the civil law tradition, derived from Roman law, as compared with the common law tradition descended from English common law.
2. However, there are many differing approaches to the theory of law, and although these may often be categorised as indicated below, there is also much blurring of the lines between them, and in some cases hardly any lines to blur.
3. Thus, although no one would be likely to argue that Kelsen (chapter 4) was not a legal positivist or Aquinas (chapter 2) a naturalist, many writers cannot be so neatly pigeon-holed, e.g.:
   - Fuller (chapter 2) occupies a more ambiguous naturalist position;
   - Hart (chapter 7) adopts a more qualified or perhaps advanced positivist stance;
   - Dworkin (chapter 7) has formulated what has been described as a 'third way' between natural law and legal positivism;
   - some writers adopt a radical political stance that is not necessarily clearly rooted within traditional boundaries, e.g. Marxists or sociologists of law;
   - others would not see themselves as subscribing to any historical categories, but within their own broad classification (e.g. critical legal studies, realism or historicism) can be just as difficult to pin down;
   - whichever legal philosophers are being studied, they are usually characterised by subtlety and complexity of language.

4. Nevertheless, some attempt at classification is needed in order to bring both the wood and the trees into focus, so after outlining the main categories and general definitions, more detailed consideration is given to some of the principal legal philosophers and their ideas and writings on legal theory.

1.1.3 General approaches

1. There are a number of broad ways of approaching jurisprudence, so legal theory may be addressed by studying (see chapter 1.2 for definitions):
   - analytical and normative jurisprudence;
   - doctrinal theory;
   - policy analysis;
   - comparative explanations and classification;
   - criticism of distinctive bodies of law;
   - comparisons of law with other categories of knowledge;
   - critical theories of law such as race or gender (see chapter 6).
2. A variant to such methodologies is to examine legal philosophy by reference to social science and humanity disciplines, some of the more usual including:
   - history;
   - (moral) philosophy;
   - political science or economy;
   - sociology;
   - anthropology and culture.
3. This may be refined to the study of more specific allied conceptual subjects such as:
   - justice;
   - punishment;
   - rights;
   - obligations;
   - equity;
   - legal personality.

4. The objective of much legal philosophical writing is to provide answers to questions such as:

- what is law, and what is its purpose?
- how does a legal system operate?
- are there sufficient common factors that can be identified to produce a general theory?
- is law something that can stand alone, or does it need to be welded to concepts such as justice or morality, or a vaguer notion of the 'spirit of the people', in order to be valid?
- stated slightly differently – is there, or should there be, any necessary nexus or connection between law (or a legal system), and subjective or cultural concepts such as rights, obligations or justice? (The important question of the difference between 'is' and 'ought' is dealt with in the following section.)

5. When legal philosophers commence their studies and write about their theories, the process is often referred to as that particular writer's 'project', thus:

- in a study of the relationship between globalisation and legal theory comprising a decade of research and essays, William Twining refers to it as his project, his purpose being to explain the phenomena he discovers and to analyse them in context;
- Aquinas's 'project' (although in his time he would not have called it such) was to explain the relationship between God's law and human law, whilst Marx's was to show that law is historically inevitable and secular.

1.1.4 'Is' and 'ought'

1. A crucial distinction that always needs to be borne in mind in jurisprudential discussion is the question of 'is' and 'ought':

- some legal philosophers concern themselves with analysis of what a particular subject *is*, which involves objective description, explanation and discussion;

- in other cases the writer will be evaluating the aims and objectives he or she considers a system *ought* to achieve, inevitably involving consideration of subjective criteria.

2. The impossibility of deriving an 'is' conclusion from 'ought' premises was highlighted by Hume, who pointed out that:
   - it is not logical to reach conclusions about what ought to happen from facts about what actually is;
   - the consequence of this is that normative or behavioural conclusions cannot follow from statements of fact (see section 3.1.4).

3. This can be demonstrated by a syllogism (see section 1.2.2 for the definition), the valid form of which is as follows:
   - all women are human;
   - Ruth is a woman;
   - therefore, Ruth is human.

4. Ethical non-cognitivism, however, leads to a fallacious or false syllogism, e.g.:
   - all pigs have trotters;
   - Brian is a pig;
   - therefore, Brian *ought to have* trotters.

5. Although it may be considered very likely that Brian will actually have trotters, it is not valid to conclude that he *ought* to have them, and this is the fallacy or false argument identified by Hume.

6. It should be noted that from an *academic* point of view it is not conclusively right or wrong, inferior or superior, to write about law as it is or as the writer considers it ought to be, but it is important that the distinction should always be clearly drawn.

7. From the *philosophical* viewpoint, however, natural lawyers argue that you cannot have a proper legal system that is devoid of religious or moral content, whilst the purer legal positivists would say that law and morals are, or should be kept, distinct and separate.

1.1.5 Natural law

1. Natural law is the theory that law can only be understood by requiring that extraneous or non-legal matters should be taken into account in determining its meaning and legitimacy.

2. These imported ideas are generally moral elements, and more specifically would link natural law to such considerations as:
   - religion;
   - morals;
   - rights;
   - reason;
   - justice;
   - conscience.

3. By implication, natural law incorporates the *overlap thesis*, the 'overlap' being the extent to which law and morality should be considered together and treated as part and parcel of each other, although opinion differs markedly as to the extent to which and the ways in which this might occur.

4. At the more intense end of the spectrum are located writers such as Aquinas and Blackstone, who in effect argue (although from different religious viewpoints) that law cannot be law if it does not accord with their notion of what God requires law to be, which inevitably involves questions of external imposition and faith.

5. However, the wide variety of religious attitudes of natural law writers means that there may be little common ground about the bases on which their natural law beliefs are founded.

6. Natural law may play an unexpected role in the formation of individual legal systems, e.g. canon or Church law was formative as one of the strands that went into (later) common law.

7. Complete legal traditions (as opposed to separate individual state legal systems) may in this sense have a natural law

foundation, such as the:

- Islamic Shari'a;
- Jewish Talmud;
- Hindu laws of Indian origin.

8. Others, adopting a less stringent overlap basis, would only suggest that there should be some minimum moral element in a legal system if it is to carry authority for those who comprise its subjects, thus implying a secular link between law and morality that need not be founded on religion.

9. Some of the more obvious difficulties concerning natural law are that:

- the origin and nature of the suggested moral input vary enormously;
- there is no agreement as to whether such input should comprise religious or secular moral values, and if religion which one and which version (think of the belief gap between Roman Catholics and Quakers);
- objective study of the natural law system itself is not enough, because external factors always have to be imported, involving either faith or some other subjective element that goes beyond scientific or rational analysis.

10. Historically, natural law can be traced back to the Greeks some 2,500 years ago, and thence via the Romans through the medieval Catholic Church to more recent centuries, when it was challenged in the post-medieval centuries by broad European intellectual movements such as the Enlightenment and Reformation.

11. In the nineteenth century it was substantially displaced by the growth of legal positivism, but has enjoyed a more limited revival in the twentieth century, partly due to the inability of positivism to justify atrocities perpetrated by regimes of supposed legal legitimacy.

1.1.6 Legal positivism

1. Legal positivism is the group of legal theories which represent the view that law comprises the rules and operative

machinery found within a state's jurisdiction, so long as it has been legitimately imposed, and in its purest or extreme sense regardless of religious or moral content.

2. Roughly it can be said to be the opposite of natural law, because it:
   - is entirely imposed (or posited, hence the name) on society by humankind;
   - need take no account of morality;
   - can incorporate whatever provisions its makers and enforcers wish.
3. It is therefore taken to refer to the many different state or municipal legal systems, e.g. the English, French, Albanian or Chinese legal systems, regardless of the wide differences between their respective aims, objectives, methodology and operational rules.
4. An example often used in this context is the legal system of Nazi Germany, drafted and imposed by a lawfully elected regime, amoral in purpose, and ultimately deadly evil in its consequences.

1.1.7 Variants of legal positivism

1. Within legal positivism there are a number of theses, including the *social fact* or *pedigree thesis* which emphasises that it is social facts that ultimately provide legal legitimacy.
2. This approach is exemplified by some of Jeremy Bentham's thinking, elaborated and developed by his disciple John Austin into the command theory, whereby a legal system is characterised by having a 'sovereign' (meaning the law maker(s) rather than a monarch) imposing law by issuing commands, whilst not being subject to any higher sovereign.
3. Later developers of the social fact thesis such as HLA Hart thought that other rules existed which provided the power to make, change or repeal such laws.
4. Hart wrote about primary and secondary rules, the secondary category comprising rules of:

- recognition;
- change;
- adjudication.

5. The *conventionality thesis* argues that any such social facts must conform to the social conventions acceptable to the society under consideration.

6. The *separability thesis* denies any necessary or constitutive relationship of law to morality, thus effectively comprising the opposite of the overlap thesis.

7. The *'third way'*, an interpretation of Ronald Dworkin's writings, emphasises the role of judges in using moral principles to decide 'hard cases', but not deriving those legal principles from social criteria.

8. There are various other approaches to understanding the nature of law, such as John Stuart Mill's *harm principle* and Lord Devlin's *legal moralism*, and differences such as these have led to famous controversies and discussions, such as the Hart–Devlin and Hart–Fuller debates.

9. These in turn led to further twentieth-century developments of legal theory, invoking responses by writers such as Jules Coleman, John Finnis, Ronald Dworkin, John Mackie and many others.

10. Although legal positivism had earlier roots, it really established itself in the nineteenth century, largely as a result of the pioneering efforts of Bentham and Mill and the work of John Austin, who later became the first professor at the newly established University of London, and their approach was continued into the twentieth century by other positivists such as Hans Kelsen.

11. The result was a decline in belief in natural law during the nineteenth century, although the horror of what a rigid adherence to legal positivism could lead to brought about a twentieth-century revival in natural law and reconsideration by some legal philosophers such as the German jurist Radbruch (chapter 2).

1.1.8 A rich tradition

1. The long jurisprudential tradition from the ancient Greeks to the twenty-first century has sometimes led to an apparently contradictory polarisation of the debate into over-wide categories, primarily natural law and legal positivism, with the more recent addition of many other developments, often originating in the new world.

2. This can result in considerable over-simplification and insistence on black and white categories of thought, but historical and cultural advances have played their part in advancing legal jurisprudence, e.g.:
   - the emergence from the Dark Ages and European educational revival;
   - the Enlightenment;
   - the Reformation;
   - scientific discoveries and improved methodology which ensued;
   - empiricism and rationalism (chapter 3).

3. However, later centuries brought about other developments in legal thought, for example the historical legal schools associated with:
   - Friedrich Karl von Savigny (1779–1861);
   - Sir Henry Maine (1822–88);
   - Sir Frederick Pollock (1845–1937);
   - Frederick William Maitland (1850–1906).

4. Marxism had an influence on legal as well as economic theory in the former Communist second world, and few would have forecast that it would be mostly discredited by the end of the twentieth century, and that the Socialist world itself would largely have plunged into the process of 'withering away'.

5. Important Marxist influences, with the influence of Marx himself, include:
   - Georg Wilhelm Friedrich Hegel (1770–1831);
   - Karl Marx (1818–83);
   - Yevgeniy Bronislavovich Pashukanis (1891–1937).

6. An American alternative, formalism or conceptualism (section 6.1), requires logical deduction of rules from a study of relevant cases in order to determine the legal principles to be derived from them, and involves treating law like science; philosophers include:
   - Christopher Columbus Langdell (1826–1906);
   - James Barr Ames (1846–1910).

7. American pragmatism (section 6.2) is represented by writers such as:
   - Charles Sanders Pierce (1839–1914);
   - William James (1842–1910);
   - John Dewey (1859–1952).

8. Realism (section 6.3) describes the subjective approach of a judge who has to make difficult decisions based on hard questions that parties bring before the court, although it developed along different lines in the United States and Europe, characterised by American and Scandinavian realists.

9. The former are represented by:
   - Oliver Wendell Holmes (1841–1935);
   - Karl Nickerson Llewellyn (1893–1962);
   - Jerome Frank (1889–1957).

10. The latter (section 6.3.6) are represented by:
    - Axel Hagerstrom (1868–1939);
    - Karl Olivecrona (1897–1980);
    - Alf Ross (1899–1979).

11. In the 1970s the critical legal studies movement (CLS – see section 6.4) emerged in the United States, and a number of branches have resulted including:
    - feminism;
    - critical race theory;
    - postmodernism, influenced by literary theory;
    - economic law theory (e.g. Richard Posner, see section 7.5.2).

12. Writers who have promoted CLS include:
    - Robert W Gordon;

- Morton J Horwitz;
- Duncan Kennedy;
- Catharine A MacKinnon;
- Roberto Mangabeira Unger.

13. These, and other aspects of jurisprudence, deserve and have
   devoted to them many theories, some of which are
   considered in this book.

1.2 VOCABULARY AND LANGUAGE

1.2.1 Jurisprudential language

1. Because of the subject matter under consideration
   philosophers, and perhaps especially legal philosophers, use
   and manipulate words and language, trying to extract the
   finest points of exact meaning out of every phrase and
   utterance, but this can sometimes in itself lead to confusion.
2. Wherever possible such fine distinctions are avoided in this
   book, so the words 'legal philosophy', 'legal theory' and
   'jurisprudence' are not meant to be construed in restricted
   technical contexts.
3. Some of the basic terms and ideas used in this book and in
   discussing legal theory are briefly summarised alphabetically
   below, and will be referred to or dealt with in more detail in
   subsequent chapters.

1.2.2 Theories and definitions

1. Theories and definitions:
   - analytical jurisprudence: studying scientifically what the
     law actually is, looking at and analysing specific legal
     systems and their structures so as to understand how
     they operate;

- *a priori*: deductive process of reasoning from known or accepted facts to an assumed conclusion, without reference to inductive experience;
- *ab initio*: from scratch, or from the beginning;
- codification: the process of making written laws, derived from either customs or pre-existing norms, or *ab initio* by a duly authorised legislature or similar body;
- cognitivism: the theory that it is possible to reach absolute and true conclusions about such things as morality and justice, acquired through perception, intuition and reasoning rather than by deduction;
- commands: characterise the imperative idea of those legal positivists (originating with Austin) who believe that legal systems must have a 'sovereign' or ruler who lays down the law but who is not subject to a legal superior (see also imperative);
- contractarian: the idea that humankind binds itself into society by a kind of (theoretical or notional rather than actual) social contract (e.g. Rousseau, section 3.2.4), agreeing to forgo some natural freedoms 'enjoyed' in a state of unbridled nature for the collective security that is derived from becoming a member of a tribe or society;
- critical legal studies (CLS): a collective name for a variety of (mostly American) legal movements emerging from the 1970s and towards the end of the twentieth century concerning themselves with such issues as feminism, race and sexual orientation, and discrimination;
- deduction: a process of reasoning by which a general conclusion is drawn from a set of premises, based mainly on experience or experimental evidence;
- dialectics: the art of reasoning, more particularly the art or practice of assessing the truth of a theory by discussion and logical disputation, especially the Hegelian debating philosophy adopted by Marxists that by juxtaposing or contrasting opposites, establishing a thesis and then locating its antithesis, a process of

synthesis will then produce new and higher forms of knowledge;

- economic analysis of law: a theory of justice put forward by Richard Posner (chapter 7) advancing the proposition that the way to achieve justice is *via* economic efficiency so that the two things are attained simultaneously by allowing people to maximise wealth or, in other words, it interprets the operation of the legal system by placing prime consideration on economic factors;
- empiricism: the doctrine that all knowledge derives from experience based on inductive reasoning and the observation of phenomena (as opposed to rationalism);
- *ex post facto*: after the event;
- felicific or hedonistic calculus: this was Jeremy Bentham's suggestion for calculating the totality of pain and pleasure within society so that the consequences and thus the worth of specific actions and choices could be worked out in advance;
- formalism: the idea that certainty rather than individual (e.g. judicial) choice should apply to legal interpretation and construction, so that words and concepts would have a fixed meaning from which deviation would not be acceptable (a strict common law approach unmitigated by equity);
- good(s): something(s) which is/are assumed (often by naturalist writers because of its subjectivity) to be (a) desirable objective(s) to be achieved or obtained in a legal system, e.g. John Finnis identifies the basic forms of human good as:
  - life;
  - knowledge;
  - play;
  - aesthetic experience;
  - sociability or friendship;
  - practical reasonableness;
  - religion;

- hermeneutic: to do with interpretation, especially but not necessarily of Scripture;
- historical school of jurisprudence: a movement that grew up alongside legal positivism in the late eighteenth and nineteenth centuries as a reaction to natural law, especially in Germany under the influence of Hegel and Savigny, and developed in England by Maitland, Pollock and Maine;
- imperative: the legal positivist idea that law derives from the commands of the 'sovereign' or ruler in a given legal system, exemplified by John Austin's adaptation of aspects of Jeremy Bentham's writings (see commands);
- induction: a process of reasoning by which a specific conclusion necessarily follows from a set of general premises;
- intuitionism: the idea that people's consciences enable them to know the difference between good and evil, right and wrong, so that they instinctively know how to behave;
- jurisprudence: the science or philosophy of law, which may be further particularised and qualified by such descriptions as historical, critical, sociological, economic etc.;
- justice: the moral principle that determines the fairness as opposed to the legality of actions;
- law: a set of rules or norms of conduct permitting or preventing specified behaviour or relationships of persons, legal or natural, with punishments and remedies according to the type of matter under consideration;
- legalism: perception of the social world in the context of legal ideas, a vital component of the Western liberal world view;
- libertarian: belief in the doctrine of free will, or an approach to legal philosophy that emphasises the idea of protection of basic personal rather than collective freedoms;

- materialism: Karl Marx wrote about the twin ideas of historical and dialectical materialism, believing that it is the material conditions of society that drive development and progress, and rejecting suggestions that nobler spiritual influences might be important to mankind;
- metaphysics: theoretical philosophy of being and knowing, or the philosophy of the mind, and in a popular sense abstract or subtle talk, or mere theory;
- morality: is at the root of the fundamental differences between the natural law and legal positivist approach to jurisprudence, concerning the distinctions between right and wrong, required to be an intrinsic part of law by naturalists and distinguished as being logically and objectively separate by positivists;
- moral philosophy: the traditional study of morality, i.e. the process of reaching moral judgments by humans striving to decide what is wrong or right;
- normative jurisprudence: considering what the law ought to be, thus involving evaluation against subjective standards, and seeking a moral element of good;
- norms: standards of social behaviour generally acceptable within a particular legal system, but used in a more technical sense by Hans Kelsen as a qualified instruction to officials to apply sanctions (secondary), prompted by a primary norm that justifies such sanction (see section 4.5);
- officials: the generic term given to persons who implement the will of the state, and so used in a wider sense than the usual English meaning to include, for example, the judiciary, police and prison services;
- ontology: the department of metaphysics concerned with the essence of things or being in the abstract;
- philosophy: the rational investigation of being, knowledge and right conduct, systems or schools of thought, and so it can encompass:
  - analytical jurisprudence, in the consideration and analysis of objective phenomena;

- normative jurisprudence, which examines and evaluates desirable attributes in a legal system;
- policies and principles: policies are the expression of desirable (legal) objectives to be achieved within society, but can be overruled by principles on occasions when there might be conflict, e.g.:
  - the policy that an heir can inherit may be overruled, when the potential beneficiary murders the testator in order to gain premature possession of his inheritance (*R v Sigsworth* [1935] Ch 89);
  - in *R v Allen* (1872) LR 1 CCR 367 a married defendant 'married' again, and argued that he could not have been guilty of bigamy as the second marriage was illegal, but to assert the desired legal principle marriage on the second occasion was treated as meaning having gone through a ceremony of marriage;
- rationalism: the doctrine that reason rather than experience is the proper basis for regulating morals and conduct (as opposed to empiricism);
- relativism: in a critical sense, the thesis that all points of view are equally valid and all moralities equally good; alternatively, it means respect for beliefs that are alien to one's own, as in cultural or ethical relativism;
- rhetoric: the art of persuasive or impressive speaking or writing, language designed to persuade or impress;
- sanction: in legal positivist theory, the pain, suffering, consequence or punishment that is supposed to be the motivating factor in persuading people to obey the law, examples being:
  - fines;
  - imprisonment;
  - community service;
  - reparation;
- sociological jurisprudence: a theoretical approach to law that treats it as a social phenomenon and so involves examination of its origins, operation and the effect it has

on society;

- syllogism: a deductive inference by which a logical conclusion is derived from two propositions, the major and minor premises (see section 1.1.4.3 for an example);
- teleology: the philosophical study of the evidence of design or purpose in nature, by which people believe that there is some purpose leading towards an inevitable conclusion, originating in classical Greek thought;
- utilitarianism: the ethical theory that the highest benefit lies in the greatest good of the greatest number, which means that the criterion of virtue is utility, promulgated by Jeremy Bentham and John Stuart Mill, and divisible into:
  - total or classical;
  - average;
  - act;
  - actual rule;
  - ideal rule.

CHAPTER 2

NATURAL LAW

Greeks: early classical naturalism: Socrates, Plato and Aristotle: Sophists, Stoics etc.	
	Romans: codes and orators: Cicero, Gaius and Justinian
Christians: Augustine and Aquinas: God-given natural law	
	Secularists: Grotius and Pufendorf: growth of humanism and international law
British Empiricists: experience, induction and probability	
	Continental Rationalists: reason, deduction and certainty
Immanuel Kant: the categorical imperative	
	Gustav Radbruch: the formula combining natural law with legal positivism
Lon Fuller: the inner morality of law: the eight principles	
	John Finnis: the seven basic goods and values of human existence

2.1 THE GREEKS: EARLY CLASSICAL NATURALISM

2.1.1 Socrates, Plato and Aristotle

1. Probably the most famous early Greek philosophers were Socrates, Plato and Aristotle, their project being to study what they perceived as the nature of things, and they identified an unchanging nature that was paramount and pre-eminent above all other things.

2. Socrates (469–399 BCE) did not leave any writings of his own, other than indirectly *via* his student Plato, but he believed that:
   - instinct was not enough to explain human nature;
   - there must be a higher power, which he thought of as reason or intellect;
   - no one does evil deliberately and if one behaves badly it is because of ignorance;
   - virtue is knowledge, and humans should be wise in everything they do in life.

3. Plato (427–347 BCE) was a disciple of Socrates and developed his thoughts and beliefs into what became known as the Platonic ideal:
   - solid things of the world are reflected in the realm of ideas;
   - justice is reflected in the notion of 'order' or harmony;
   - the orders of Greek society were the:
     - guardians or rulers;
     - military;
     - artisans or workers;
   - this was in turn reflected in the three parts of the human soul, namely:
     - rationality;
     - appetite;
     - spirit.

4. Plato's great work was *The Republic*, which took the form of a dialogue in which he used various characters to represent differing points of view, by asking questions of the sort that his own teacher Socrates had used (hence the 'Socratic' Q & A method of teaching).

5. Aristotle (384–320 BCE) believed that:
   - the nature of a thing is its end, and he looked to human nature for answers to philosophical questions;
   - mankind achieves knowledge by learning about its own nature, hence the aphorism (summary of the principle) expressed as *Know Thyself.*

6. His main works were *Ethics* and *Politics*, which were based on the fundamental premise that all men act for some good and that their end in life is to do good.

7. He wrote about the four 'causes', which he identified as:
   - matter;
   - form;
   - agent;
   - end.

8. By 'end' he meant the whole activity of man as established in the form of human nature, and the need to achieve fulfilment by completion of a person's development.

2.1.2 Other Greek movements and ideas

1. The Sophists preferred to use argument or rhetoric rather than these kinds of detailed theories of knowledge, so they developed and perfected the art of persuasion and became famous orators, exemplified by:
   - Protagoras of Abdera;
   - Prodicus of Ceos;
   - Hippias of Elis;
   - Gorgias of Leontini, who said that he did not need to know about a subject in order to be able to answer questions about it.

2. By Plato's time there had developed some prejudice against the Sophists, and by Aristotle's time the word had become something of a term of abuse.

3. The Stoics developed a theory of natural law that used as its basis some of the ideas of Plato and Aristotle, believing that natural law is:
   - right reason in agreement with nature;
   - of universal application, unchanging and everlasting;
   - impossible to abolish;
   - unalterable, and that to try to change it would be sinful.

4. Their ideal man was one guided through his life by reason, citizens of the then known world equally at home in the Persian (Iranian), Hellenistic (Greek) or Roman civilisations, and more particularly they:
   - believed that their gods were identifiable with the forces of nature;
   - were tolerant of people who worshipped other gods (pantheism);
   - were scientists, believing in a universe designed in accord with divine reason and governed by divine providence, the purpose of mankind being to live a good life in accordance with natural laws;
   - had a keen sense of duty, which later came to be reflected in the ideals of the Romans.

5. Sceptics were exemplified by Pyrrho (c. 365–275 BCE) and believed that real knowledge of things is impossible.

6. Epicureans took their name from Epicurus ((341–270 BCE) and believed that the highest good is to seek pleasure or freedom from pain, a philosophy that resurfaced in the nineteenth-century ideas of the utilitarian movement.

2.2 THE ROMANS

1. The Romans had considerable interest in adapting and developing Greek ideas to benefit the expanding Roman Empire because:
   - there was general belief in some kind of all-pervading 'natural' (therefore by implication universal) law;
   - the Romans had conquered most of the known world, so they could administer that law everywhere, with as much Roman flavour as they could manage.

2. They believed in and developed a number of ideas including:
   - *ius naturae*, almost the same idea as the law of nature, meaning a law supported by natural reason, i.e. it should also be a law applicable to all nations, thus acting as a support for *ius gentium*;
   - *ius gentium* or the law of nations, used to describe the laws that the Romans found common to different states, as opposed to their own municipal laws, although it was also used in a different sense to mean those laws that applied both to citizens and foreigners;
   - *ius civile*, on the other hand, was the main body of Roman civil law that originally only applied to Roman citizens.

3. Cicero of Arpinum (106–43 BCE) in *De Republica* said that:
   - true law is right reason in agreement with nature, diffused among all men, constant and unchanging;
   - to curtail that law is unholy, to amend it illicit, and to repeal it impossible;
   - all men could therefore potentially be equal in reason and understanding before that law, even if not in their material and human circumstances.

4. Cicero is credited with combining the Stoic idea of a universal law of nature directing the course of human conduct, with the psychological attitude of the Sceptics, thus adapting the Greek tradition (for which he had great respect) with that of the Romans.

5. Marcus Aurelius (121–80 CE) followed the Stoic tradition, and was credited with reforming the laws to remove some of their contradictions and severe consequences, for the benefit of minors, women, and slaves.

6. Gaius (or Caius) (130–80 CE) was a jurist of the Sabinian school who wrote his *Institutes* about 161 CE, and although not famous in his own times became so later because his work was subsequently used in a number of different ways and for a variety of purposes:
   - as a student textbook because of the clear way it explained the law;
   - as a model for classifying the law into a tripartite or three divisional system comprising the law of:
     - persons;
     - things;
     - actions;
   - by Justinian several hundred years later as the basis of his own *Institutes*.

7. Justinian (527–565 CE) is remembered for a number of important and influential legal works, and he:
   - organised and gathered together all the imperial statutes into a comprehensive *Codex Constitutionum*;
   - compiled a *Digesta* or *Pandecta* of the writings of other Roman jurists;
   - wrote a student textbook called *Institutiones* or *Institutes*;
   - enacted new laws under the title of *Novellae*.

2.3 EARLY CHRISTIAN NATURAL LAW

2.3.1 St Augustine: a continuing tradition

1. One of the problems of trying to understand early jurisprudential ideas is the lack of continuity in written sources, but despite this traditions continued and developed

and the links are there even when they cannot always be easily traced.

2. Towards the end and after the fall of the Roman Empire Christian influence grew and spread throughout the known world, and much of the philosophy of classical natural law was amenable to the Catholic Church, once it had been adapted to replace classical pantheistic ideas of multiple gods with one Supreme Being.

3. Saint Augustine of Hippo (354–430 CE) was one of their greatest bishops and philosophers, and his works included *Confessions* and *Retractations, On Free Will,* and *The City of God.*

4. As a Catholic theologian he was able to fuse Platonic philosophy with revealed dogma, but with the emphasis on Christianity wherever the two came into conflict (this came to be known as Christian Platonism).

5. In *De Civitate Dei* (*The City of God*) he tried to show the human condition struggling against the forces of evil, pulled in contrary directions by good and wicked people.

6. So the highest or eternal law is the will of God, with mankind's positive law something of a lower order, whose purpose is merely to keep people in order.

7. In 1140 CE the Catholic Church gathered together a version of Canonical law that provided the early medieval conception of what was meant by the law of nature (the *Decretum Gratiani,* the oldest collection of Church law embodied in the *Corpus Iuris Canonici*).

8. It was believed that mankind is ruled by two types of laws, natural law and custom, natural law being that which is contained in the Scriptures and the Gospels.

9. This concept of Christianised natural law formed the main basis of jurisprudential belief from the fifth century throughout the middle ages, and continued more or less unchallenged in the Western world until the intellectual developments of the post-medieval Enlightenment and Reformation led to serious opposition and questioning of accepted beliefs.

2.3.2 St Thomas Aquinas

1. In the early part of the second millennium Saint Thomas Aquinas (1225–74 CE) was probably the leading exponent of Christian natural law (Thomist philosophy), as explained in his book *Summa Theologica*.

2. He classifies law into four categories:
   - eternal law, comprising divine reason which can only be understood by God, constituting His infinite and unknowable universal master plan;
   - natural law, which mankind is able to discover by the use of reason, and which involves participation in God's eternal purposes;
   - divine law, the law that God has imposed on mankind which is learnt from the Bible;
   - human laws, i.e. those imposed by temporal authorities on their subjects for their overall benefit, which are:
     - designed to deal with the realities of the world;
     - required to keep people in order and punish them for committing crimes;
     - necessary to regulate the various legal relations that need to be controlled;
     - recognition of what some six centuries later would become the subject matter for the Bentham/Austin command theories of positive law, the rule-based derivatives of Hart, and other twentieth-century developments of this precursor of legal positivism.

3. Law to Aquinas is rational regulation for the good of the community, made by the person(s) having powers of government and promulgated or published, which is what provides the positivist element.

4. His idea of moral law may be described as the general principle that all finite beings move towards their ends by the development of their potentialities, which is sometimes referred to as Christian Aristotelianism.

2.4 SECULAR NATURAL LAW

2.4.1 Continuity and change

1. It is not practical to detail and do justice to all the writers and philosophers who went on subsequent to the thirteenth century to develop natural law theory, for a number of reasons:
   - there were religious and secular versions, which themselves varied considerably;
   - the single thread of growth that can be traced from Greek *via* Roman to early Christian subsequently divided into many factions;
   - the timescale involved covers some 2,500 years from the early Greeks to the present day.

2. The persistence in combining religion (and by implication morality) with law when considering the essential requirements for a legitimate legal system meant that the scope of the subject widened as the centuries passed.

3. A few of the more influential writers who had things to say about natural law and related philosophy in the sixteenth to eighteenth centuries include:
   - Hugo Grotius (Huigh De Groot) (1583–1645) (see section 2.4.2);
   - Samuel, Baron von Pufendorf (1632–94) (see section 2.4.3);
   - John Locke (1632–1704) (see section 3.1 under empiricists);
   - Jean Jacques Rousseau (1712–88) (see section 3.2 under rationalists);
   - Sir William Blackstone (1723–80);
   - Immanuel Kant (1724–1804) (more of a moral libertarian philosopher, but with much to say about natural law);
   - Thomas Paine (1737–1809) (more an early exponent of natural rights rather than natural law).

4. Broadly based natural law beliefs could be held by both continental rationalists and British empiricists, as can be seen from chapter 3, the differences stemming as much from their approach to knowledge as the conclusions they reached.

2.4.2 Grotius

1. Hugo Grotius, a Dutchman, is acknowledged as being one of the founders of international law, but also played a seminal role in the development of natural law thinking.
2. His contribution was to break the connection which insisted that God (in his case the Calvinistic God) was the necessary and only source of ethics and morality, so, in a phrase, Grotius based natural law on human nature, rather than on religion of any kind.
3. He wrote seminal works setting out these principles, including:
   - *Mare Liberum* (*Freedom of the Seas*) (1609), the theme, as indicated by the title, being that the seas cannot belong to anybody or any nation;
   - *De Jure Belli ac Pacis* (*On the Law of War and Peace*) (1625), in which he drew on earlier Spanish philosophers such as Francisco de Vitoria (1483–1546) and Francisco Suarez (1548–1617).
4. In some ways Grotius reflects the Romans in his development of natural law ideas, bringing together a number of influences in order to formulate his legal philosophy:
   - consideration of the secular and divine;
   - the effects of war and peace;
   - trade and the necessity for maintaining freedom of the seas.
5. He distinguished between primary and secondary laws of nature, in this particular perhaps reflecting Aquinas:
   - primary laws are those that entirely express God's will;
   - secondary laws are those that comprise rules of behaviour coming within Man's reason.

6. Much of his consideration of the nature of law was undertaken in the context of his interest in international law, war and the settlement of disputes, which he believed could be resolved by:
   - negotiation between opponents;
   - compromise, or settlement;
   - confrontation, or allowing fate to determine outcomes;
   - justice, the important element required in dealing with dispute, which brings about a peaceful conscience.
7. His insistence on there being a close relationship between law and morality influenced later writers such as Pufendorf, Blackstone and John Locke, for example in Locke's *Two Treatises on Civil Government* published in 1689.

2.4.3 Pufendorf

1. Samuel, Baron von Pufendorf was a German jurist and historian who like Grotius studied international law and believed that the law of nations is:
   - not to be treated as positive law imposed by Man;
   - natural law, based on the idea that human beings are social animals;
   - rooted in the idea that the natural relationships between nations should be peaceful, so that war can only be considered as a last resort.
2. He also reflected Grotius in giving primacy to secular rather than religious legal authority, foreshadowing the way that Church and State would later operate in Germany.

2.4.4 Blackstone

1. Sir William Blackstone's influence through his *Commentaries on the Laws of England* took some of the natural law ideas initially away from continental Europe to Britain, and thence to America, influence he shared with John Locke (see section 3.1.2).

2. His basic project was to produce a comprehensive account of the common law, but indirectly this affected legal education and claims to natural rights, and his notion of natural law was religious rather than secular or humanistic.

3. In utilising these ideas in the American Declaration of Independence and thence into the Constitution, Thomas Jefferson combined the two in the phrase 'law of nature and of nature's God'.

4. This fusion can be seen in the persuasive and memorable wording used:
   - self-evident truths;
   - all men created equal;
   - endowed by the Creator with certain inalienable rights;
   - Life, Liberty and the pursuit of Happiness.

5. Blackstone's contribution to the origins of these ideas comes in his *Commentaries* where he writes about personal security, the elements of which were:
   - enjoyment of life, limb, body, health and reputation;
   - that it is a gift from God;
   - that it is a right inherent by nature in every individual.

6. Elements of Blackstone's natural law beliefs are reflected in other areas of practical law, e.g.:
   - taxation;
   - property rights;
   - self-defence (the American right to bear arms, which they believe constitutes an essential element of freedom).

7. Despite exerting all this influence, it should be emphasised that Blackstone was fundamentally opposed to the American insurrection, sitting as a monarchist Member of Parliament from 1761 to 1770, but nevertheless his naturalist common law writings were adapted and used by those fighting for freedom.

2.4.5 Kant

1. Immanuel Kant (1724–1804), one of the world's greatest thinkers since the time of the ancient Greeks, provides a

development from and contrast with classical and religious natural lawyers, stating that:

- the only original right that belongs to Man by virtue of his humanity is freedom, i.e. not being restricted by the will of any other person;
- actions are right provided they accord with other people's freedom;
- to acquire and own property there should be general consent (in contrast to Locke who thought that ownership of vacant property could be acquired by 'mixing' one's labour with it).

2. Kant took the view that the content and methodology of empiricists and rationalists (see chapter 3), in their attempts to escape the human mind to attain knowledge of the world, were wrong:

- empiricists because of their belief in the senses which is *a posteriori* reasoning;
- rationalists because of their use of *a priori* reasoning, not relying on experience to reach conclusions.

3. His critical philosophy is found in his *Critique of Pure Reason* (1781), which dealt with the bases and categories of human knowledge, the *Critique of Practical Reason* (1788), and the *Metaphysics of Ethics* (1797).

4. One way of examining propositions is by dividing them into:

- analytic, i.e. self-evident, so that truth can be gleaned by studying the subject in question;
- synthetic, i.e. something that cannot be arrived at by pure analysis, thus requiring experiential input.

5. Another method is to split them into:

- empirical, i.e. depending on the perception of human senses;
- *a priori*, i.e. not requiring such perception.

6. Kant was much exercised by ethical ideas, believing that actions should be dictated by a sense of duty guided by reason, leading to two imperatives, the:

- hypothetical imperative, where the action taken leads to a specific end or objective;
- categorical imperative, which is the basis of human morality and which should therefore inform the law;
  - 'imperative' means that it is a command or instruction;
  - 'categorical' means that there can be no exceptions or ways of avoiding the command.
7. This imperative, as addressed to the individual trying to decide on proper behaviour, is:
   - 'act as if the maxim of your action were to become through your will a general (or universal) law of nature';
   - thus the means can never justify the end;
   - the right thing to do is one's moral duty because it is one's moral duty, not because one thinks it is the right or most enjoyable thing to do.
8. Kant has been enormously influential as a philosopher, changing and developing the terms of earlier debate and having a great effect on Hegel, who in term influenced Marx.

2.5 DECLINE AND REVIVAL

2.5.1 Nineteenth and twentieth centuries

1. In the nineteenth century there was a marked decline in the potency of the natural law movement, much of which can be put down to the growth of other influences, e.g.:
   - Jeremy Bentham (1748–1832), with his crusade for radical legal reform and utilitarianism;
   - John Austin (1790–1859), who systematically developed Benthamite ideas into legal positivism (see chapter 4) and more specifically the command theory;
   - John Stuart Mill (1806–73), hugely influential in the implementation of utilitarianism;

- various other influential Victorian philosophers and
  writers, such as Thomas Carlyle and Matthew Arnold.
2. Belief in natural law never faded away completely, however,
   given its strong association with religious beliefs and its
   insistence on combining law with morality.
3. In the twentieth century there was a revival of interest in
   natural law, characterised amongst others by the writings of:
   - Gustav Radbruch (1878–1949);
   - Lon Fuller (1902–78);
   - John Finnis (b. 1940).
4. The distinction between natural law and legal positivism
   varies according to the fervency of belief of particular
   writers:
   - at one end of the spectrum are those who seem to be
     unable to recognise that anything other than natural law
     is conceivable;
   - at the other end are those who refuse to recognise a need
     for any moral or religious input to validate a secular legal
     system, if it is legitimately installed and operated;
   - a wide range of intermediate views that can incorporate
     elements of both, by distinguishing and defining
     particular limiting factors;
   - examples of these might include HLA Hart's rule-
     based approach to legal positivism, and Ronald
     Dworkin's 'third way'.
5. One point of view is that during the course of the twentieth
   century aspects and precepts of natural law have developed
   into human rights, a process that can also be traced back to
   the eighteenth-century American and French revolutions,
   which in turn has origins in Locke, Blackstone and others.

2.5.2 Radbruch

1. The German legal scholar and former Weimar Minister of
   Justice Gustav Radbruch engaged in a debate with the
   English philosopher HLA Hart after the Second World War,

which went to the core of the meaning of natural law, the questions under consideration being:

- is law necessarily connected to morality?
- can 'evil' (Nazi) law be considered to be law proper?
- if law is immoral, or to some extent 'sufficiently' immoral, how can it be treated as being valid?
- if it is possible to categorise law as 'evil' or 'wrong', where does that leave the question of obedience to law?

2. Legal positivist advocates, at their most extreme, argue that law cannot be immoral, so it would:

- always have to be obeyed, thus having the effect of legitimising the laws of the Third Reich (or in this century Myanmar or Zimbabwe);
- justify the legality of Nazi legislation and judicial decisions;
- also have the effect of nullifying the *post hoc* creation of the international war crime of genocide, and the Nuremburg and Tokyo War Tribunals.

3. Radbruch took the line that it is better to decide that 'evil' legislation cannot be law, in turn making it clear to officials that superior orders cannot be a defence or justification.

4. Hart was more concerned with achieving conceptual perfection, rather like Kelsen – this point of view paid less attention to potential consequences.

5. Radbruch was thus seen as changing from a strict legal positivist pre-war stance to one that accepted some influence of natural law, given the obscene consequences of legal positivism carried to extremes.

6. His conclusion is summarised by what came to be known as *Radbruch'sche Formel* or Radbruch's formula, which states that statute law must be disregarded by a judge where it:

- is incompatible with the requirements of justice to an extent that it becomes intolerable, or;
- was clearly designed in a way that deliberately negates the fairness and equality that is central to all justice.

7. In a more specific practical context, German courts dealt with cases after the Second World War that had to address

real hard questions, along the lines later suggested by Dworkin, e.g.:

- a wife was prosecuted for denouncing her husband for making derogatory remarks about Hitler under 1934–8 anti-sedition laws, trying maliciously to get him executed, although he was sent to the Eastern front instead and survived;
- she was convicted on the basis that she herself had committed the crime of illegally depriving another person of his freedom under the 1871 German Penal Code.

8. These are examples of how natural law concepts revived in the twentieth century, for a number of reasons and in different ways:

- the boundaries blurred whilst at the same time the debate matured and became more complex and sophisticated;
- natural law became identified with natural rights, especially after the atrocities of the Second World War had fuelled the human rights movement;
- Hart continued his law and morality debates later with Lon Fuller and Lord Devlin.

2.5.3 Fuller's inner morality of law

1. Lon Fuller (1902–78) occupies some part of the middle ground between pure legal positivism and natural law:

- opposing legal positivism and criticising Kelsen, Hart and Dworkin;
- advocating a species of 'secular natural law' in *The Morality of Law* (1964);
- engaging in debate with Hart, discussing the relationship between law and morality with regard to the:
  - nature of law;
  - meaning of legal language;
  - question of whether wicked or immoral law could properly be regarded as law.

2. Fuller suggests there is an inner morality or order for law, whilst Hart believes in the separation of law and morality.
3. From Hart's position (although he did to some extent qualify this) it would follow that a legal system can be valid even though it is immoral, and taken to extremes racist, sexist or other discriminatory laws formally passed by a legitimate regime would *ipso facto* have to be regarded as legitimate.
4. Fuller argues that after the Second World War it was legitimate for courts to decide that Nazi law was in some respects illegitimate, because morality cannot be completely divorced from the content and operation of the legal system.
5. Thus Fuller sees the need for a connection between law and morality by means of reason (e.g. the *ex post facto* creation of the crime of genocide to punish Nazis for what had not been illegal under Third Reich laws, even though they were always morally unsatisfactory and unacceptable).
6. The need for a legal system is to produce rules for governing people's behaviour that are consistent with the moral objectives of society, which leads to what he calls 'the inner morality of law', internal to the system because they are a necessary intrinsic application of the morality behind it.

2.5.4 Fuller's eight principles

1. He summarised these ideas as comprising eight principles:
   - there must be known and ongoing rules of conduct expressed in general terms, not random orders or instructions;
   - the rules must not be retrospective, as it would be wrong to punish or disadvantage people for crimes or breaches of law for things which were not wrong or illegal at the time they were done;
   - publication of the rules is essential so that people know in advance what they are and what is expected of them;
   - rules have to be intelligible, expressed in terms that are

understandable, so they must be clear, obvious and unambiguous in their meaning;

- the rules should be consistent and not contradictory;
- it must be possible for people to obey the rules, as it is pointless to have laws which the public are unable to obey;
- this also means that laws should remain as constant as possible, as frequent changing of rules leads to uncertainty and inability to keep up with the law's requirements;
- the administration of the rules should be consistent, the officials applying and enforcing them being obliged to behave in a manner that conforms to their content.

2. These principles in their totality are necessary before any set of rules can be considered to constitute a proper legal system, and it is this that makes the principles 'internal' to the legal system.

3. The requirements are aspirations and some legal systems may operate better or worse according to the degree to which they may or may not take to heart all the principles.

4. Opponents of Fuller such as Hart argue that it is not necessary for the principles to be 'moral' as such, but for Fuller a legal system that does have these driving principles behind it will in any event be a moral one.

2.5.5 Finnis's basic values and principles

1. John Finnis (b. 1940) sets out to explain in *Natural Law and Natural Rights* (1980) what he considers to be the basic:
   - values of human existence;
   - principles of all practical reasoning.

2. He does this by considering:
   - how such values and principles enter into any consideration of good reasons for action, and any full description of human conduct;
   - the sense in which such basic values are what he calls self-evident.

3. The basic values he identifies are:
- Life, which:
  - corresponds to the drive for self-preservation;
  - signifies every aspect of the vitality of life;
  - includes cerebral health and freedom from pain and injury;
- Speculative knowledge, which is:
  - desirable for its own sake;
  - not a means to an end;
- Play, engaging in performances that have no point beyond the performance itself, enjoyed for its own sake, which may be:
  - solitary or social;
  - intellectual or physical;
  - strenuous or relaxed;
  - highly structured or relatively informal;
  - conventional or *ad hoc* in its pattern;
- Aesthetic experience, beyond elements arising out of Play, which thus:
  - seeks out beauty externally or by inner experience, or;
  - arises through the act of creating some work in a significant or satisfying form;
- Sociability (or friendship), which involves acting for the sake of one's friend's purposes and well-being, rather than for oneself;
- Practical reasonableness in using one's intelligence to choose one's actions and lifestyle, and to shape one's character, thus requiring complex values and involving:
  - evaluation, preferences and hopes;
  - self-determination;
  - freedom and reason;
  - integrity and authenticity;
- Religion, involving the relationship between the other basic but transient goods and cosmic eternity.

4. Finnis is at pains to explain that:
- 'basic goods' does not mean moral good;
- there are many other goods, but on analysis they turn

out to be ways or combinations of pursuing goods from
his primary list of seven;
- there are other virtues which are not basic values, such as
courage and generosity, but they are ways in which basic
goods are or are not pursued;
- all the basic goods are equally fundamental, so there is
no order of precedence to them.

2.5.6 *Natural Law and Natural Rights*

1. In *Natural Law and Natural Rights* Finnis also considers a
number of other matters, including:
   - justice;
   - rights;
   - authority;
   - law;
   - obligations.
2. He says that his concept of justice embraces three elements:
   - other-directedness, concerned with one's relations and
dealings with other persons;
   - duty, that which is owed or due to another person,
corresponding to what that other person has a right to;
   - equality, but in the sense of proportionality rather than
in an arithmetical sense.
3. He partially defines his theory of justice negatively in that
unlike Hart it is not restricted to:
   - treating like cases alike and different cases differently;
   - the basic institutions of society;
   nor to his ideal conditions of a society in which everyone
complies fully with the principles and institutions of
justice.
4. There are three important aspects of justice:
   - general justice, the concrete implications of the basic
requirements of practical reasonableness;
   - distributive justice, ensuring resources are shared fairly in
the wide sense of:

- opportunities;
- profits and advantages;
- roles and offices;
- responsibilities;
- taxes and burdens;
- commutative justice, comprising the range of reasonable responses to secondary problems concerning what is required for individual well-being within the community.

5. Rights means human rights, in Finnis's terms the modern way of explaining natural rights, the words being used by him to mean the same thing.

6. In his essay 'On the Incoherence of Legal Positivism' Finnis demonstrates that he appreciates elements of positivism whilst denying its overall validity, as the binding character of law cannot be explained by positivism.

CHAPTER 3

EMPIRICISTS AND RATIONALISTS

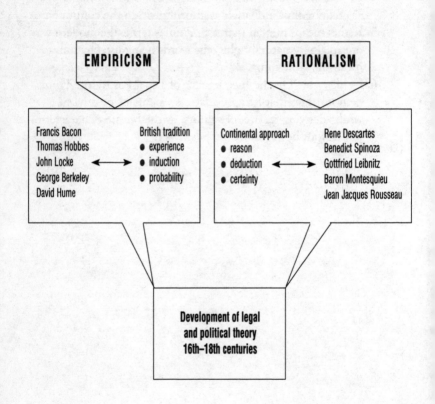

3.1 EMPIRICISTS

3.1.1 British tradition

1. Influenced by the Renaissance, philosophers tended to focus on human nature and the law of nature, but not in the same ways that classical and medieval thinkers had done.

2. There was no longer such concentration on a direct consideration of God as being the centre of the universe, because men knew by this time that the earth itself was not the centre of the universe either.

3. Interest grew in discoveries and the advancement of material science, with increased knowledge of physics, astronomy and mathematics, a seminal English influence being Sir Isaac Newton (1642–1727).

4. The resulting scientific advances had a considerable *methodological* effect on legal philosophy, with much of the emphasis being redirected to collection of empirical data on the premise that, if it produced such exciting results for pure science, it could also be adapted to progress the social philosophical science of jurisprudence.

5. The idea was that it is not the soul that provides the explanation of how mankind operates, but a constantly changing and developing collection of perceptions flashing across the brain, linked to some kind of association with the mind, an early anticipation of psychology.

6. These were all influences that took strong root in Britain, the methodology to be used being empiricist, and its main characteristics and key words being:
   - experience;
   - induction;
   - probability.

7. Important British empiricists included:
   - Francis Bacon (1561–1626), whose *Novum Organum* is an exposition of the inductive method of interpreting nature;

- Thomas Hobbes (1561–1626), who is usually remembered for describing Man's existence as solitary, poor, nasty, brutish and short;
- John Locke (1632–1704), whose best-known work is entitled *An Essay Concerning Human Knowledge* but who also wrote influentially on government and rights;
- George Berkeley (1685–1753), whose views changed considerably during his lifetime, but who ended up believing that the only realities were God, the soul, and ideas in the human mind;
- David Hume (1711–76), who wrote the *Treatise of Human Nature* explaining that all ideas are derived from sense impression, which he called the phenomena or appearances of things reflected in the senses;

8. Of these and many others, perhaps the three most influential were Hobbes, Locke and Hume, an interesting comparison being that whilst the three rationalists dealt with in section 3.2 influenced English jurisprudence, those English philosophers in turn heavily influenced Europe and America.

3.1.2 Hobbes

1. Thomas Hobbes (1588–1679) was a philosopher whose view of life as a pessimistic writer was coloured by a number of things as he:
   - was born in the same year as the Spanish Armada attempted to conquer England;
   - lived through mostly depressing times, including the English Civil War;
   - died in extreme old age.

2. Influenced by Galileo's ideas on perpetual motion, he originally intended to write a comprehensive account of science, men and citizens, but was obliged to take refuge on the continent.

3. Eventually he published his important work *Leviathan* in 1651, expanding on an earlier work *De Cive* (*On the*

Citizen) published in 1642, in which he argued that:

- Man is selfish, self-interested and pursues his own good at the expense of others;
- such unenlightened self-interest pursued in ignorance would lead to disaster;
- society in a state of nature would negate any possibility of civil order or rule of law;
- given these characteristics of human existence, Man's life would inevitably be 'solitary, poor, nasty, brutish and short', a 'war of every man against every man'.

4. However, there are some positive counter-balances, including the fact that:

- people possess a right of nature, i.e. a wish to survive;
- they have a degree of rationality, or law of nature;
- the right of survival at all costs that justifies a person's violence has to be renounced in order to achieve mutual security;
- this leads to a rough state of uncomfortable balance in society.

5. What is needed, therefore, to guarantee stability is a 'Leviathan' (in this context a person or body of formidable ability, power or wealth) who must provide the basis for a social contract, which may be either:

- an absolute monarch, or;
- a democratic parliament.

6. The Leviathan is given absolute power in return for securing peace and stability for its citizens, so if power is the sole element that legitimates the law:

- it is the act of rebellion that is wrong rather than supporting one form of government or another;
- values such as justice, morality, freedom and property have no universal or eternal meaning, being dependent upon the policy of Leviathan;
- the state is always right as long as it is achieving its primary objectives of stability and maintenance of peace.

7. His discussion of what he identifies as the nineteen laws of nature can be reduced to the following basic rules:

- men should strive to keep the peace;
- they should be prepared to give up much of their right of nature in return for protection;
- generally they should follow the golden rule of 'do as you would be done by'.

8. In summary, Hobbes' philosophy contains:
  - aspects of natural law;
  - social contractarian elements;
  - some of the ideas of legal positivism, in a disregard of the need for morality, freedom, justice etc.;
  - suggestions of utilitarian hedonism;
  - perhaps most of all, and explanatory of the others, pragmatic responses to contemporary difficulties, or an early form of realism;
  - a counter-balance to more optimistic traditions of legal thinking;
  - an argumentative inclination to enter into philosophical disputes, reminiscent of HLA Hart in the twentieth century.

3.1.3 Locke

1. John Locke (1632–1704) led a varied earlier life, mixing the occasional practice of medicine and involvement in political intrigues with experimental science and travel, obtaining extensive political experience working for the Earl of Shaftesbury followed by high administrative offices, and so developing his interest in government.

2. Major key points in his natural rights philosophy are:
  - the existence of a benign state of nature, but without organisation;
  - need for a compact or social contract (cf. Rousseau), where each person resigns himself into the hands of the community;
  - a method of government by consent;
  - people retaining the right to resist tyranny (i.e. the right

to revolt, which translated perfectly for the purposes of the American revolution);
- the intrinsic right to property, obtained by 'mixing' or using one's labour.

3. His expression of natural rights was the phrase 'life, liberty and estate', which became transformed in the American Declaration of Independence into 'life, liberty and the pursuit of happiness'.

4. Relatively late in life he published *Two Treatises of Government* and *Essay Concerning Human Understanding* (1690), although he had been working on the latter for some twenty years.

5. The *Essay* is divided into four parts, dealing respectively with:
- innate principles, demonstrating his dislike of them;
- ideas;
- words;
- knowledge.

6. The *Two Treatises* have a closer bearing on legal philosophy, his objectives being to:
- refute the doctrine of the divine right of kings;
- produce a justification reconciling liberty for the individual citizen with the power of the state.

7. Although Man does not rule in a state of nature, there nevertheless exists God's moral law, which means that:
- men must work to justify their ownership of property, which they then hold with the consent of government, because of the scarcity of resources;
- government is therefore required because of the need of a social contract between governors and governed, to replace the freedom that everyone possessed in a state of nature;
- the social contract only grants limited power to government, and the people who grant that power can impose obligations and withdraw or modify it as they choose.

3.1.4 Hume

1. David Hume (1711–76) is of special interest because he was the person who perhaps best articulated the *is/ought* question that is at the root of understanding legal positivism (see section 1.1.4).

2. He argued that whatever knowledge we could gain from how things operate (i.e. matters of scientific or provable fact), that cannot lead directly to behavioural or normative conclusions about how things ought to be, because such conclusions would amount to a logical fallacy.

3. Because something *is* does not mean that it *should* or *ought to be*, and taking this view means that his philosophical position was to oppose much of what natural law represented.

4. Hume also denied that there is any difference between moral and other judgements, adopting a strongly empirical and sceptical viewpoint, later to be developed and reflected in the writings of Bentham and in Austin's teachings.

5. *A Treatise of Human Nature* follows Bacon and Descartes in that it is sceptical about religious and metaphysical idols, which are replaced by certain truths which:
   - cannot be derived solely from pure reason;
   - require observation and experience of the empirical self.

6. However, trusting that 'self' leads to a confusion of impressions and emotions, and an imagined perception of identity.

7. Nevertheless the facts of the world are and have to be taken in *via* our senses, which are part of ourselves, and not to be trusted for the reasons just given, so Hume says that leaves us with alternative choices, either to:
   - retreat into a passive disbelief in everything, admitting a helpless inability to do anything faced with the problems of the world, leading to nervous and social breakdown, or;
   - use a common-sense approach as represented by human understanding of common life.

8. In order to do this it is necessary to work within a tradition, as all knowledge and enterprise originate in traditions, even though this does not and cannot lead to absolute and certain truth, and we can only use the methodology of our traditions and guess at truth and answers.

9. So, rules of law, morals, justice and such qualities are the result of our historical traditions and experiences, and we should be slow to change things when someone suggests an appealing idea such as the notion of equality.

10. The conclusions to be drawn are that we:
    ● search for knowledge of the actual operation of the world by gathering empirical facts;
    ● use them as a guide to how we construct our society, and how we should behave.

3.2 RATIONALISTS

3.2.1 Continental approach

1. In continental Europe a rather different path was being followed, which was termed rationalism, whose adherents believed a more appropriate and preferable method of obtaining knowledge should be founded on reason rather than the investigation of empirical data.

2. Human reason, it was argued, works without the assistance of Divine revelation, although it was accepted that some assistance comes from the senses.

3. This was based on a different interpretation of how science could be used, as in both cases the motivating inspiration came from pure and practical (as opposed to social) scientific developments.

4. Key words for rationalists, rather than the experience, inductive methods and probability of the empiricists, were:
    ● reason;
    ● deduction;
    ● certainty.

5. Important continental rationalists included:
- Rene Descartes (1596–1650)
- Benedict (Baruch) Spinoza (1632–77), whose book *Ethics Demonstrated in a Geometrical Manner* (*Ethica Ordine Geometrico Demonstrata*) (77) attempted to show that what Euclid had done for geometry he could do for the rest of human knowledge;
- Gottfried Leibnitz (1646–1716);
- Christian Wolff (1676–1754);
- Baron Charles Montesquieu (1689–1755);
- Jean Jacques Rousseau (1712–88).

6. Of the rationalists, the three who had the greatest influence on English jurisprudence were perhaps Descartes, Montesquieu and Rousseau.

3.2.2 Descartes

1. It is a basic belief of rationalism that truth can be discerned *via* the senses, so the famous saying of Rene Descartes (1596–1650) '*Cogito ergo sum*' (I think therefore I am) sums up the core of his rationality.

2. Cartesian metaphysical dualism, considered in his *Meditations* published in 1641, is the belief that:
- mind and body comprise two separate and distinct classes of substances;
- each is able to have causal effect on the other;

3. This implies that there must be:
- thinking substance *(res cogitans)*, referring to the human soul and its relationship to God;
- extended substance *(res extensa)*, meaning the corporeal world.

4. Rational methodology involves application of logical, mathematical and scientific principles to philosophy, e.g.:
- nothing should be accepted as true unless it is clear and distinct;
- problems should be split and divided into component parts, to make analysis easier;

- straightforward ideas should first be considered and progression then made towards complexity;
- it is vital that all stages of a problem be considered and nothing omitted.

3.2.3 Montesquieu

1. Baron Charles Montesquieu (1689–1755), in *The Spirit of the Laws* published in 1748, describes, amongst other things, how positive laws are founded on a state of nature.
2. Natural justice is something objective that he believes exists, and is not dependent on human nature.
3. He follows the Greeks in thinking that the state's *raison d'être*, i.e. its basic justification, is to provide a system of justice, so it follows that:
   - natural law is the law of reason;
   - positive law provides specific examples of the application of natural law;
   - this allows for a variety of differing man made laws from one state to another.
4. Montesquieu's four laws of nature are more or less the opposite of Thomas Hobbes' account of mankind's existence (solitary, poor, nasty, brutish, short), comprising:
   - peace;
   - need for food;
   - the procreative drive;
   - the social drive.
5. He was also responsible for developing the doctrine or theory of separation of powers, based on the belief that the branches of government should be divided into the:
   - legislature, i.e. Parliament, the maker of laws;
   - executive, i.e. the Crown or government, enforcer of laws;
   - judiciary, i.e. the judges, interpreters of laws.
6. This was necessary because if law-making powers were available to the same person or group of people who were responsible for law enforcement and interpretation,

despotism would reside in the same place, and no liberty would be possible.

3.2.4 Rousseau

1. Jean Jacques Rousseau (1712–88) advances in his early writings the idea of the social drive when he attacks and criticises the evils of society and civilisation, arguing that:
   - mankind is basically good – a noble savage occupying a state of nature;
   - the cause of people's unhappiness is artificial and corrupted society.
2. In his *Discourse on the Arts and Sciences* (1750) he says that the advancement of art and science has not been a good thing for mankind, as it makes governments more powerful and individuals less free.
3. He suggests a return to a state of nature, which he sets out in his book *A Discourse on the Origin and Foundation of the Inequality of Mankind* in 1755.
4. In his later work *The Social Contract* published in 1762 he:
   - modifies his views to some extent, arguing that the development of society is necessary to overcome the rough and inequitable conditions that a state of nature inevitably entails;
   - attempts to find a political formula that would maintain in society what he still sees as the benefits of being in a state of nature, i.e. liberty and equality.
5. His law of nature is more grounded in mankind's instincts or feelings than on reason, the driving force behind behaviour being, after the primary instinct for self-preservation, a sentiment of compassion for other human beings.
6. From that flow many other worthwhile values that reflect the goods identified and desired by twentieth-century writers such as John Finnis, in particular:
   - friendship;
   - generosity;

- the essential positive characteristics of humanity itself.

7. The well-known opening words of *The Social Contract*, sometimes wrongly attributed to Karl Marx, sum up Rousseau's philosophy, where he says that 'Man is born free; and he is everywhere in chains'.

8. In other ways, however, he does foreshadow some of the views of Karl Marx and Friedrich Engels, criticising the institution of private property and claiming that the purpose of government should be to ensure justice, education and equality for everyone in society.

9. Even so, his main thrust is founded in natural law, emphasising the importance of freedom and morality in political and legal systems.

3.3 GENESIS

1. These mostly seventeenth-century philosophers, whether empirical or rational, shared a number of important characteristics:
   - they were often interested in a wide range of subjects, not restricting themselves purely to writing about legal theory;
   - some of them played important practical roles in their respective societies, thus influencing thought and action directly as well as theoretically;
   - despite living in difficult times, they were brave and usually unreserved in seeking out and proclaiming the truth as they saw it;
   - they were also instrumental in laying the foundations for a number of crucial later developments in political and legal terms, including the:
     - French and American revolutions in the latter half of the eighteenth century;
     - rediscovery and restatement of the tenuous doctrines that had arisen from time to time in previous writings

but which emerged as full-blown legal positivism in the nineteenth century;

- theoretical discussion that would provide the basis for the current liberal world picture of human rights as the successor to natural rights.

2. They constituted vital continuity in the development of post-medieval legal philosophical thought through the Enlightenment and Reformation and onwards into Victorian and modern times, in this way proving to be the genesis or birth of the modern age.

CHAPTER 4

LEGAL POSITIVISM

Auguste Comte:
three-stage development
of human laws:
invention of social science
of sociology:
scientific methods

Jeremy Bentham:
utilitarian rejection
of natural law:
development of unique
language: complex
theoretical legal system

Legal positivism: laws
imposed by Man on
society: rejection
of God and morality as
being essential for a
legal system

Hans Kelsen:
a pure theory of law:
avoidance of 'pollution'
of other social norms
and the *grundnorm*

John Austin:
categories of law
determined: proper
and improper: law
based on obedience and
sovereignty:
command theory

4.1 COMPARISONS WITH NATURAL LAW

1. As a general guide, the natural law school of philosophy judges the validity of law by:
   - reference to religious or moral criteria;
   - ideas derived from subjective beliefs rather than objective data;
   - requiring outside factors and considerations to be brought into the subject matter under discussion.

2. In its purest form, legal positivism takes an opposite view to that of natural law, so that it:
   - examines and assesses a legal system on the basis of the law applicable to a particular society, i.e. within a defined jurisdiction;
   - only considers laws imposed and operated by valid human machinery;
   - ignores moral criteria;
   - is only incidentally concerned with justice;
   - assesses the particular municipal law under consideration by reference to sanctions, rules, principles and conventions;
   - is legally posited or imposed (this is where 'positivism' comes from, rather than implying the opposite of negative).

3. However, in practice, much legal positivistic thinking does implicitly accept an element of moral influence in the imposition of law, whilst still maintaining that law and morals are two different and distinct concepts, on the practical basis that law would barely work if it was contrary to the generally accepted morality of the society in question.

4. Legal positivism is therefore based on an express or implied acceptance of the principle of moral relativism, which:
   - does not acknowledge absolute human moral and behavioural standards;
   - does recognise cultural, religious, social and other differences.

5. In simple terms, moral relativism says:
   - there can be no ultimate set of moral principles that apply to all persons at all times;
   - changes are bound to occur in the way that people understand and justify beliefs and behaviour, resulting from (amongst other things):
     - the passage of time;
     - their stage of social and political development;
     - their religious viewpoint, or absence of such beliefs;
     - material considerations such as affluence, class, security etc.;
   - this reflects the views of the Greek Sophists, who believed that Man is the measure of all things, and were doubtful of being able to discover anything that was really objectively true.

6. So two broad and different views of human life lie behind the traditional natural law and legal positivist theories, with natural law:
   - relying on an initial intuitive hypothesis about the nature of law;
   - reaching conclusions from this to arrive at a definite explanation of that nature.

7. Problems with natural law are that the initial hypothesis may be inappropriate, or affected consciously or subconsciously by the ideological beliefs of the person who believes in that theory.

8. On the other hand, legal positivism does not concern itself with extraneous moral or religious considerations, but concentrates on the legitimacy of the man-made laws that apply to the particular society under consideration.

9. Problems with legal positivism are that it can lead to simplistic conclusions about the legitimacy of law within a particular society that have no bearing on the non-legal outcomes that people expect from their laws, which (depending on the society and amongst other possible criteria) may include:

- justice;
- democracy (of which there are many variations);
- rights (and obligations);
- remedies (compensation or equitable, e.g. injunction);
- maintenance of established religion;
- economic and social redistribution.

4.2 COMTE

1. Auguste Comte (1798–1857) was one of the main philosophers whose ideas led to the rapid growth of legal positivism in the nineteenth century, and he is also credited with the invention of sociology, meaning the scientific investigation and analysis of society.
2. He believed that the highest form of human knowledge relates to the simple description of sensory phenomena, basing his ideas on a three-stage evolutionary law in which the following steps are identified:
   - Stage 1 is theological, where human beings explain the natural events with which they are confronted by reference to anthropomorphic wills:
     - 'anthropomorphism' means attributing human form or behaviour to animals or deities, and so would equate to chthonic (pronounced 'thonick') systems of law;
     - 'chthonic' means laws as perceived by aboriginal, native or indigenous peoples, the origins of which are lost in the mists of time, and still relevant in some parts of the world, e.g. Australia and New Zealand in a Western context, and the Amazon Basin in a primitive context;
   - Stage 2 is metaphysical, during which these wills are depersonalised, and essences or forces (such as the force of nature) are used to explain phenomena:
     - 'metaphysical' means in a general sense the system of first principles and assumptions underlying an inquiry of a philosophical nature;

- Stage 3 is positive or scientific, and is the final development:
  - at this stage men and women accept that understanding of the events they experience are best achieved through the processes of inductive and deductive reasoning;
  - in a sense this combines the methodology of the empiricists and rationalists – see chapter 3.
3. Legal positivists are so described because, through an observation of legal phenomena, they arrive at a definition of law based on actual experience, rather than attributing it to an unseen God or deities, human nature, morality or other imponderables.

4.3 BENTHAM

4.3.1 Bentham's wide influence

1. Jeremy Bentham (1748–1832) pursued philosophical interests such as utilitarianism that were very much wider than the conventional limits of jurisprudence, but nevertheless his influence on legal positivism was considerable, principally through his disciple John Austin, so it is important briefly to consider that input.
2. His writings are enormously complex, so much so that at one point HLA Hart, who was editing some of his work, doubted that he had the technical expertise to unravel much of its meaning.
3. Bentham rejected ideas of natural law and claims that it had any internal qualities, famously referring to the French revolutionaries' constitution as 'nonsense on stilts and bawling on paper'.
4. He did not accept notions of God's will in the sense that Augustine and Aquinas believed in it, but replaced them with the idea that law is an assemblage or collection of signs expressive of the sovereign's subjective will.

5. The sovereign is the person or body who is obeyed in a given political community, whose members have the habit of obedience to a person or body above them.
6. Sovereignty thus means:
   - in its first strict and proper sense, a traditional monarch;
   - under a secondary formulation and what he calls an improper sense, the person or body which is all powerful and must be obeyed, but which is not subject to any higher authority (so in the United Kingdom, comprising the legislative process, that is the Queen in Parliament).

4.3.2 Language and ideas

1. Bentham also writes about:
   - 'aspects' of the law, i.e. the various forms it can take, such as commanding, allowing, permitting etc., in order to achieve its objectives;
   - 'extent' of the law – how widely and to whom it is to be applied, e.g. criminal law extends to sane adults but within society there will be:
     - legally immune citizens such as minors and patients under the Mental Health Acts;
     - persons subject to disabilities, such as prisoners;
   - 'mandates', or the legitimacy and status of various actions undertaken within society, e.g.:
     - instructions issued by employers to employees;
     - orders given by parents to children;
2. Distinctions can be drawn between:
   - expressions of will that can be imperative in the form of commands;
   - prohibitions that require adherence;
   - permissions that do not prevent one from doing something and which can therefore be construed as allowing action.
3. Primary law governs behaviour, but secondary or subsidiary law has to be established to identify and punish breaches of criminal law or rectify matters under the civil law.

4. This, however, suggests additional subsidiary levels of law to govern officials such as judges, the police and the prison service.

4.3.3 A system of law

1. Bentham tried to devise a complete system of law comprising the totality of the subsidiary and principal laws within a stated system in order to give life and meaning to the general principle, exemplified as follows:
   - there is a general prohibition against meddling with other people's property;
   - more specifically, therefore, we are not allowed to occupy another's property, i.e. this is a prohibition, which is imperative;
   - however, the same situation can also be regarded as a permission, allowing anyone who has a good title to occupy the land or use the property;
   - following this, there must be recognised procedures to transfer, validate and register property, with mandates and penalties to ensure compliance;
   - taken together, these comprise a complete law, although Bentham would accept that it cannot all be reduced to writing and set out in this precise form;
   - it follows, therefore, that the owner of property under English law has two different kinds of power;
     - first, legal permission to use the property, which Bentham calls 'contrectation';
     - second is the consequence that other people cannot use the property unless they have the owner's permission, which he calls 'imperation'.
2. Although these are difficult ideas, language and concepts, their influence in the development of legal positivism on John Austin, especially the command aspects, was considerable, and Bentham's more general philosophy was also crucial in the growth of utilitarianism.

4.4 AUSTIN

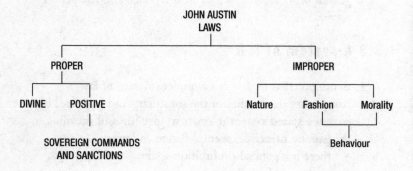

4.4.1 Austin's influence

1. John Austin (1790–1859), often described as Bentham's 'disciple', was influential in the growth of legal positivism and was appointed first professor of jurisprudence at the newly established University of London in 1826.

2. After much research in Germany his first lectures were delivered in 1828 and subsequently published under the title of *The Province of Jurisprudence Determined* in 1832.

3. He was not particularly successful in getting his ideas accepted during his lifetime, despite support from influential people such as John Stuart Mill, partly because he was meticulous in trying to ensure that his meaning was absolutely clear, so giving the impression of being excessively pedantic.

4. He was trying to produce a system of general principles of jurisprudence that would necessarily be part of any system of law, a theory of the nature of law uncontaminated by notions of morality or religion, and that could be applied in all contexts.

5. The legal rules that he identified are those addressed by (a) political superior(s) to political inferiors, at the same time distinguishing positive law from rules that, whilst similar in nature or related by way of analogy or metaphor, are in fact quite different.

4.4.2 Categories of law and morality

1. A fundamental distinction to make is between laws proper and improper.
2. Laws proper comprise two sub-classes:
   - divine law;
   - positive law.
3. Laws improper constitute:
   - laws by analogy (e.g. the 'laws' of fashion);
   - laws by metaphor (e.g. the law of nature and positive morality).
4. The positive law argument is then developed through the command theory of law, through:
   - notions of duty;
   - enforcement by sanction;
   - the role of the sovereign.
5. Positive morality takes three forms, comprising:
   - rules of behaviour, which exist in societies that have not yet developed institutions of government and are still in a so-called state of nature;
   - rules laid down by sovereigns not acting in their capacity as such;
   - rules intended to regulate human behaviour which owe their origins to the thoughts and beliefs of individuals, but which are not necessarily enforced by institutions of government.

4.4.3 Command theory

1. A command is one means by which a desire can be expressed and distinguished from other means of expressing will by the power of the commanding party to inflict evil or pain in the event of the desire not being fulfilled, i.e. punishment for disobedience.
2. Giving a command imposes a duty on the person to whom it is directed, and so 'command' and 'duty' are correlative terms (compare this with Wesley Hohfeld's analysis of rights

in section 6.1).

3. The 'pain' attendant on failure to carry out a command is a sanction.

4. The source of positive law is to be found in the activities of the sovereign body, and the existence of an independent sovereign state implies that sovereignty relies on three factors, i.e. that:

   ● the bulk of the society concerned are in the habit of obeying or submitting to a common and determinate superior, i.e. one who can be identified, who may be an individual or group of persons;

   ● that person or group are not themselves in the habit of obeying the dictates of another human superior;

   ● the powers of the sovereign are not subject to legal limitation.

5. It is important always to bear in mind that 'sovereign' does not necessarily mean 'king' or 'queen', but the legitimate body that makes laws, which may be democratically elected although in some legal systems could gain power in other ways.

6. The attraction of this theory is its relative simplicity compared with the difficulties of understanding the complexities and wider scope of Bentham's writings.

4.4.4 Advantages and disadvantages

1. Various disadvantages and criticisms have been identified regarding Austin's development of legal positivism from the initial theories of Comte and Bentham, including:

   ● the fact that reference to a sovereign might imply a moral dimension;

   ● it may not be appropriate to define law by reference to the state (which owes its origin to the law, rather than *vice versa*);

   ● not all laws are backed by sanctions (e.g. constitutional or procedural rules, or international law);

- laws are often obeyed by citizens, not because they are afraid of punishment, but because they are by and large accepted as reasonable;
- public international law does not seem to have validity under Austin's theory, in the virtual absence of compulsory legal machinery and effective sanctions;
- it is often difficult to identify the sovereign body, especially where the doctrine of the separation of powers applies (see Montesquieu in section 3.2.3);
- his theory appears to be rather more applicable to statute-based legal systems than to those that rely more heavily on case law (which seems rather odd, writing as he did within the common law tradition, although he was influenced by German law);
- his account gives an over-simplified view of the nature of political society;
- if examined in terms of global legal systems or families, he was not addressing himself to some of these, e.g. religion-based legal systems such as Shari'a or Talmudic law.

2. Austin's writings have been much analysed and questioned, leading to attempts to adapt his views to a more comprehensive and realistic account of how legal systems work, for example the rule-based approach of HLA Hart (see section 6.3).

3. However, Austin was not saying that this was the only way of looking at law, nor that other factors such as morality are unimportant.

4. Positive law is one element, but needs to be considered alongside the laws of God and positive morality, by which he meant man-made behavioural rules of conduct, sport, etiquette, manners and so on.

5. He was concerned to set out principles that would have universal significance and application, so he referred to 'principles, notions and distinctions' in order to be able to bring in a sufficient degree of subtlety to his theory, indicating that examples of these would be the:

- notions of Duty, Right, Liberty, Injury, Punishment, Redress;
- various relations of the above qualities to the Law, Sovereignty and Independent Political Society;
- distinctions between written or promulgated, and unwritten or unpromulgated law (promulgate means to proclaim or make laws known).

4.5 KELSEN

4.5.1 Kelsen's objectives

1. Hans Kelsen (1888–1973) combined a European civil (Roman law based) approach to the study of law with his later experience of American common law in a unique and clinical approach to legal theory.
2. The first edition of his *Pure Theory of Law* was published in 1934 and the second revised edition in 1960.
3. His project, according to his translator, was to:
   - construct a pure theory of law, comprising an explanation of legal phenomena untainted by political, moral, economic or other extraneous considerations (i.e. restricted to law and ignoring other disciplines);
   - solve fundamental problems of a general legal theory in a manner consonant with principles of methodological purity of jurisprudential cognition (i.e. to extract clear basic principles);
   - locate the position of the science of law in the overall systems of sciences;
   - attempt to achieve a broad clarity of purpose that, however, is not always immediately apparent within the complexity of Kelsen's text and ideas.
4. Like Austin, his concern was to show law as it is and not as it ought to be, one of (if not the) most important characteristics of legal positivism (see David Hume, section 3.1.4).

5. It should also be emphasised that:
- he was not considering any specific legal order but a theory of positive law in general;
- the process involved removal of 'polluting' or 'adulterating' twentieth-century elements such as psychology, sociology, ethics and political theory;
- this is rather like removing the flesh and organs from a body in order to see the elegant bone structure of the skeleton that holds it all together;
- he is not denying the existence of social and other such elements, but his objective is to avoid getting them mixed up in his discussion so that the clear and philosophical truth can be seen through the social scientific fog.

4.5.2 Norms

1. Kelsen is therefore always looking at the effect achieved rather than the intention desired, e.g. the:
- subjective meaning of the act of writing one's will may not be the same as the objective meaning;
- proper legal formalities (such as witnessing the testator's signature) may not be observed, and if so the will cannot have the desired effect;
- exchange of letters between merchants may or may not have the physical effect of creating a contract, whatever the intention of the parties to the correspondence, depending on the actual rules of contract formation.

2. This approach requires first of all identification of the physical act or physical facts, whose objective meaning may be an effective or ineffective act in civil law, or a legal or illegal act in criminal law.

3. It is not the physical existence as such of the facts that turn them into legal acts, but the objective meaning resulting from human interpretation of what has happened.

4. This legal meaning derives from what Kelson calls a 'norm' whose content refers to the act, and it is the norm that confers legal meaning on the act, with the act itself being interpreted according to the norm.

5. In other words, as Kelsen says, the norm functions as a scheme of interpretation:
   - the norm which decides whether an action is legal or illegal is in turn derived from another norm;
   - thus, killing a person who has been condemned to death by due judicial process is not murder, and has a different quality to the killing that the murderer himself committed, even though the physical event of killing may well be identical, such as causing death by hanging.

6. The visual sense may not see the difference between the two, but the thought process of applying the criminal law to the execution has the effect of converting it from an unjustified random act of violence into a positive and legitimate legal action.

7. So, a norm is something that ought to be or ought to happen, and more specifically it means that a human being ought to act in a particular way.

8. The difference is:
   - in the use of the future tense as opposed to the conditional or modal;
   - the individual who commands says that something will happen;
   - the person commanded ought to behave in a certain way;
   - there is a linguistic difficulty here in that the English language does not have a direct future tense but creates the future tense by using the auxiliary verbs 'will' or 'shall';
   - it is the norm that corresponds to a command rather than to permission, and the norm is the meaning of an act by which certain behaviour is commanded, permitted or authorised.

9. Norms may derive from legislation or custom, and the effectiveness of the norm is not the relevant question so far as Kelsen is concerned, but its validity.

10. Where there exist two contradictory norms that attribute a different objective meaning to the same act, Kelsen would:
    - take a relativist view if there are two legal systems;
    - deny that there can be two contradictory valid views within the same system.
11. An example would be a robber band operating within a society that has the power to force obedience but which lacks proper legal validity.
12. Norms can eventually be traced back to a *grundnorm*, a fundamental or basic norm from which all others derive their effectiveness, and it is the existence of a socially organised coercive sanction in respect of legal norms that distinguish them from moral norms.
13. In its simplest formulation, the *grundnorm* in the English legal system can be expressed as the Queen in Parliament, i.e. the process by which new legislation is enacted and validated (debates in the two Houses followed by the granting of Royal Assent).

4.5.3 Criticisms

1. There are a number of criticisms that can be made of Kelsen's pure theory of law:
    - the *grundnorm* should not be seen as the ultimate benchmark of a legal system because the *grundnorm* itself has to be recognised by those exerting power within the society concerned;
    - a legal system is not merely a set of rules, but comprises wishes, doctrines, principles and standards that cannot necessarily all be traced to a *grundnorm*;
    - the English legal system is highly dependent on conventions and doctrines that are sometimes difficult to pin down and which can be flexible in operation (e.g. interpretation of the 'rule of law' to justify house arrest without trial, or of international law in waging war)

2. Kelsen's theory is not concerned with what the law ought to be, and he therefore accords validity to systems of rules that some people might consider to be morally indefensible:

- in attempting to provide an analysis of law that is untainted by ideological, historical and cultural bias, it might be argued that insisting on neutrality is itself a political stance, and so can be interpreted as an attack on natural law;

- other criticism can been made on the ground that his theory is so rarefied as to be virtually inaccessible, and that to exclude the social element of law is in effect to render it meaningless;

- a real problem may be encountered in trying to identify the *grundnorm* of any given legal system, although Kelsen sidesteps this by arguing that it is really a juristic supposition which does not actually require existence capable of proof.

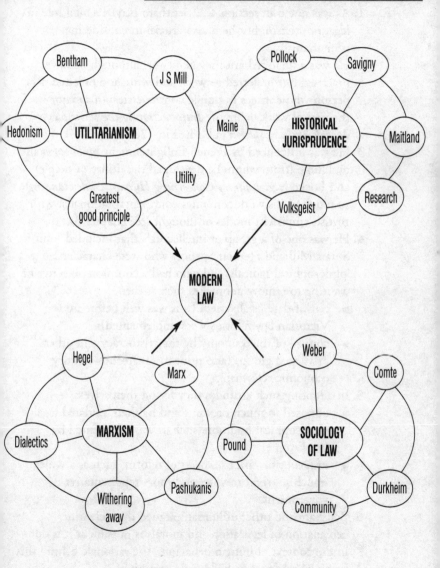

5.1 UTILITARIANISM

5.1.1 Bentham

1. As was noted in section 4.2, Bentham played a vital role in legal positivism, but he is also crucial in considering utilitarianism;

2. He was a qualified attorney (solicitor) although he never practised but preferred to work and write as a polemicist (a person who engages in public controversies), his major theoretical work being the *Introduction to the Principles of Morals and Legislation* published in 1789.

3. He was influenced by French Enlightenment *philosophes* and by Hume (from whom he developed the utility principle) and Locke (e.g. *Enquiry Concerning Human Understanding*), so much of his work combines continental rationalist with British empiricist modes of thought (see chapter 3).

4. He was one of a group of intellectuals that included John Stuart Mill and Herbert Spencer who were characterised as 'philosophical radicals' and who had a common objective of wanting to remove anomalies such as the:
   - out-of-date legal system (this was well before mid-Victorian law reforms were implemented);
   - control of the economy by the aristocracy and other privileged groups (also prior to nineteenth-century economic reforms).

5. In adopting such attitudes they found themselves:
   - opposed to much previous and by then outdated legal philosophical tradition, such as was represented by Blackstone;
   - in favour of various aspects of reform, such as a wider franchise (right to vote) and more representative government.

6. Bentham and other utilitarians argued that scientific explanation of legislation and morals is possible if it is done in the context of human behaviour, the rationale behind this being in crude terms hedonistic, meaning:

- enjoyment of pleasure;
- fear of pain;
- achievement of the greatest benefit for the greatest number of people.

7. Both can be measured by objective criteria with regard to their constitutive elements, although they themselves might be subjective or objective, such as:
   - intensity;
   - duration;
   - certainty;
   - proximity;
   - fecundity;
   - purity.

8. He also believed that people's standards of right and wrong were related to such contradistinctions and qualities.

9. It is possible to identify three principles or characteristics that make up the main bases of Bentham's philosophy:
   - utility, or the greatest happiness principle, by which he meant that which promotes pleasure, rather than usefulness;
   - universal self-interest;
   - artificial identification of the individual's interests in comparison with those of others.

10. There are a number of benefits to this way of thinking, the main one being that the utility principle is clear and obvious, and it:
    - assists decision making where conflicts of interest arise;
    - tends to human equality, one man being worth the same as another;
    - lends itself to actual calculation of interests, known as the hedonistic or felicific calculus.

11. Bentham's belief in utility prompted him to lead the way in a number of fields, e.g.:
    - he foreshadowed Hohfeld (see chapter 7) in recognising negative liberty as being freedom from external compulsion or restraint;

- he recognised rights, but distinguished them from traditional natural rights which he regarded as perversion of language;
- rights cannot be such if everyone can claim them willy-nilly (hence his attack on the French version as anarchical and 'nonsense upon stilts').

12. Rights can therefore be identified as being:
    - legal rather than natural;
    - specific both as to object and subject;
    - available only in the context of a legally imposed system, thus providing the basis for legal positivism rather than traditional natural law.

5.1.2 Mill

1. John Stuart Mill (1806–73) was subjected to intensive education by his father, James Mill, and learned about Bentham's works when he was 16 years of age, resulting in his instant conversion to utilitarianism.
2. He wrote widely on politics, economics, philosophy, culture and liberty, and published *Utilitarianism* in 1863.
3. Although deeply steeped in Benthamite utility, he recognised that it was in some ways narrow because of its empiricism, so he consciously drew on a wider perspective through other *genres*, such as Coleridge's poetry.
4. Mill also bought to utilitarianism an understanding of logic, saying that moral theories adopt one of two distinctive approaches to reach the utility principle:
   - intuitive, the Kantian way which does not depend on experience, or;
   - deductive, where the methodology required is observation and experience, preferred by Mill.
5. Pleasure can operate and be assessed by a wide range of measures, but intellectual happiness is superior to sensual happiness.
6. Summarising, *Utilitarianism* deals with the doctrine in five stages:

- first, a general introduction identifying the alternative intuitive and deductive tracks;
- second, formulation of the basic utilitarian principle that actions are right in proportion as they tend to promote happiness and wrong as they tend to produce the reverse of happiness;
- third, considering what constitutes the ultimate sanction of the utility principle, i.e. people's motivation for acting as they do, by assessing and comparing degrees of self-interest;
- fourth, producing logical proofs of his ideology and an analysis of what goes into making the complex and composite notion of happiness;
- fifth, making the connection between justice and utility, where he argues that the morality of justice is based on social utility.

7. Hedonism (the doctrine that pleasure is the highest good), self-interest, pleasure, avoidance of pain and unpleasantness all reflect the Greek philosophical movement of the Epicureans (see section 2.1.2) and may sometimes be dismissed as entirely unjustifiable because of the fact that the principle motivation is always taken to be self-interest.

8. However, when compared with beliefs that *prima facie* appear to have at bottom the unselfish motivation of universal welfare and improvement of mankind (such as Marxism) (see section 5.3.1), utilitarianism holds its own as an important factor contributing to modern world liberalism, which appears to have seen off the threat of domination by world communism.

5.2 HISTORICAL JURISPRUDENCE

5.2.1 Savigny

1. Friedrich Karl von Savigny (1799–1861) was one of the founders of the European historical school, which believed it

was important to study the will and shared consciousness of different people to understand the real nature of their laws.

2. It was necessary to discover the people's spirit (*Volksgeist*), and positive law is based on their common consciousness, the two keys to understanding thus being *people* and their *spirit*, the latter differing from one folk to another.

3. He based this on a deep study of Roman law, and his historical approach is evidenced in his work *Of the Vocation of Our Age for Legislation and Jurisprudence* (1814), in which he opposed the then Germanic trend towards codification of the law (because of Napoleonic influence).

4. The *Volksgeist* reflects what people need as the true basis of their laws, based on their history, experience, current conditions and aspirations.

5. From a legal point of view the roots of national consciousness originate in customs, although this approach goes against European continental rationalism.

6. Such a developed system required lawyers and judges to represent and interpret the law on behalf of the people in a role somewhat akin to trusteeship.

7. In practical terms he was opposed to the effects of the French Revolution and its teachings, which is one of the reasons he based his views on what he considered to be the eternal values of the Roman past's *Corpus Iuris* and the contemporary spirit of the German people.

8. Criticisms of von Savigny are based on a number of factors including:
   - the illogicality of relying and basing theory on Rome's legal past whilst at the same time arguing for a contemporary German *Volksgeist*;
   - failure adequately to define his terms;
   - over-reliance on the importance of custom;
   - the idea that lawyers operate as trustees for the people;
   - the inutility of his ideas of historical investigation to justify law, which placed more importance on origins than current law and practice;

- twentieth-century discrediting of some of the ideas because of Nazi misuse of law in the 1930s and 40s, and South African apartheid misuse of the Boer version of *Volksgeist* in the 1950s and 60s.

5.2.2 Maitland

1. Frederick William Maitland (1850–1906) was a Cambridge lawyer, closely associated with historical legal research and editing, numbering amongst his achievements:
   - the founding of the Selden Society whose purpose is to publish early English legal documents;
   - publication of Henry de Bracton's *Notebook* and the *Year Books of Edward II*;
   - authorship with Sir Frederick Pollock of *The History of English Law before the Time of Edward I*;
   - a number of other books on Equity, common law forms of action, and constitutional history.
2. Although he is perhaps better described as a legal historian rather than a legal philosopher, his scholarly adherence to researching, publishing and explaining original historical sources contributed to the strength of historical jurisprudence in the latter part of the nineteenth century.

5.2.3 Pollock

1. Sir Frederick Pollock (1845–1937) was Professor of Jurisprudence at Oxford, and brought a different balance to the English historical school from Maitland, with whom he co-operated in the publication of *The History of English Law before the Time of Edward I* and he:
   - published standard works on *The Principles of Contract* (1876) and the *Law of Torts* (1887);
   - was editor of the *Law Quarterly Review* between 1885 and 1919 and Editor in Chief of the *Law Reports* from 1895 to 1935;

- became a judge of the admiralty court of the Cinque Ports from 1914 onwards;
- was interested in other jurisprudential subjects, writing a monograph on Spinoza in 1880.

5.2.4 Importance of the historical schools

1. These lawyers, together with other nineteenth-century writers including Sir Henry Maine (1822–88), attached importance to historical methodology as explaining the spirit or essence of particular legal systems, and through the study and analysis of history coming to wider conclusions about the nature of law, and this reinforced the fact that many earlier philosophers had also taken history into account, without necessarily making it a central component in their legal philosophy.

2. Maine believed that there were a number of elements that constituted a legal system which gave it its validity, such as:
   - tradition;
   - consent;
   - mutual advantage.

3. Fairness within a legal system was therefore achieved by a process of contract rather than the existence of status.

4. In continental civil law systems Roman law was always important, and also within the English legal system as taught in the ancient universities, despite the different direction taken by the common law starting with the Norman Conquest.

5. Education for practice in the common law (as opposed to being part of a classical university education for the ruling class) was always practical rather than academic, mostly in chambers until the 1830s and the founding of Austin's Chair at the new University College of London.

6. Both the continental and English historical schools tended to reject, or at least to downplay, the supposed:
   - universality of natural law, whether based on God, gods

or a vaguer morality, whose rationality depended on intuitivism;
- neo-rationalistic explanations offered by nineteenth-century legal positivism, whether based on Bentham and Mills' utilitarianism or Austin's command sovereignty.

7. Rather, the historical schools:
- had more in common with the Romantic movement in the attempt to pin down the spirit of different peoples;
- acted as an alternative, if never a counter-balance, to the decline in natural law and growth in legal positivism;
- provided a different perspective to the growing American influences of formalism and realism.

8. There may be a number of reasons why greater success for the movement has not been achieved, in that it:
- discounts the contemporary importance given to human rights, as successor to natural rights;
- gives limited importance to moral elements generally;
- provides many, alternative, and sometimes contradictory explanations about the nature and content of legal systems;
- has suffered twentieth-century discrediting from Nazi and Boer behaviour and practices.

5.3 MARXISM

5.3.1 Hegel

1. Georg Wilhelm Friedrich Hegel (1770–1831) belongs to the post-Kantian period of German philosophical idealism, and he took an ontological and teleological approach to philosophy (for the meanings of these see section 1.2).

2. Obviously, from his dates of birth and death, Hegel was not a Marxist, but his ideas played an important part in Marx's thinking.

3. Although Hegel's writings are interpreted in a variety of different ways, it was the teleological aspects of his work that particularly influenced Marx into developing his historical

materialistic communist creed, and during the twentieth century Hegel's ideas continued to support Marxist and existentialist theory.

4. Marx used particular aspects of Hegelianism to support his work, e.g. Hegel's disagreement with Adam Smith's diffusion of general plenty (in modern terms, the 'trickle-down' effect) and to support ideas such as:

- abolition of individual ownership;
- removal of hereditary advantages;
- socialising the means of production;
- most importantly, the methodological use of Hegelian dialectics (see section 1.2).

5.3.2 Marx

1. The theory of Karl Marx (1818–83), as indicated, is rooted in the radical humanist Hegelian dialectic, but influenced by sociological factors he came to believe that legal and political structures and practices grow out of economic conditions, which led to the materialistic theory of history that coloured his later writings.

2. Although he was born into a middle-class Jewish family, he spent some time in Paris, where he was living during the 1848 revolutionary period, and thereafter he spent much of the remainder of his life suffering ill-health and living in poverty in London, where experiences of the extremes of Victorian society must have coloured his thinking.

3. He helped to move philosophy forward from the theoretical to the practical, saying that the point of philosophy should no longer be to interpret the world, but to change it, by understanding and using history, sociology and economics.

4. Specifically, he believed in historical materialism, now understood to mean the application of Marxist science to historical development, his basic proposition being that it is not men's consciousness that determines their existence but their social existence that determines their consciousness.

5. Dialectic materialism is the belief that change comes about

through the juxtaposition of contradictory ideas, a dialectic being an exchange of propositions (theses) and counter-propositions (antitheses) which lead to synthesis, and is a way of understanding reality from the differing viewpoints of thoughts, emotions and the material world.

6. Marx identified a number of stages of historical development, the more important ones being feudalism, capitalism and socialism, each stage comprising a thesis that prompted its opposite, the antithesis, and which he believed would eventually lead to an ultimate socialist synthesis where the previous organs of oppression would have withered away, leaving an ideal classless society.

7. Other well-known names such as Friedrich Engels and Lenin are associated generally with Marxism, but perhaps the most relevant writer on the legal aspects of Marxist theory was Pashukanis.

5.3.3 Pashukanis

1. Yevgeniy Bronislavovich Pashukanis (1891–1937) emerged from a group of writers including Nikolai Krylenko and Piotr Stuchka in the decade after the Russian Revolution in 1917 as the most influential Marxist legal philosopher, largely because of his treatise *The General Theory of Law and Marxism*, published in 1924.

2. He criticised previous theory such as that of Stuchka on the basis that he had failed to distinguish between legal and other social relationships.

3. Instead he thought that equivalence based on commodity exchange was the factor that identified the differentiation.

4. Marxist consideration of law was based on a dilemma comprising a number of premises, namely that:
   - tsarist laws had to be replaced;
   - this could not be achieved overnight;
   - a revolutionary philosophy had to be developed to accommodate law within state policy which provided a workable judicial system;

- within these parameters, the question of how justice might be achieved needed to be considered.

5. Legal tradition was well entrenched, which meant that legal revisionism had to be guarded against, as indeed other forms of revisionism that bedevilled the development of socialism in the twentieth century.

6. Practically, this meant:
   - restriction or control of judicial power, so that the furtherance of state objectives would not be impeded;
   - guarding against a 'restorative tendency';
   - drafting restrictive codification that would achieve these objectives;
   - specifically refusing to recognise any kind of absolute legal capacity or any inalienable and subjective private rights.

7. In *The Marxist Theory of Law and the Construction of Socialism* published in 1927, Pashukanis:
   - bemoaned the fact that Soviet law remained under the influence of dogmatic legal positivism resembling the dogmatism of natural law;
   - raised questions about the basis of Marxist law, and the socio-economic purpose of civil legal rights;
   - considered some of the practical difficulties encountered in framing and operating an appropriate legal system, e.g. of claiming compensation for injury or benefits for the unemployed.

8. In his limited objective of showing the connection between social division of labour expressed as a commodity, and the basic concepts of public and private law, Pashukanis was reasonably successful.

9. But the eventual objective was the 'withering away of the law' in a similar manner to the envisaged eventual withering away of the totality of state apparatus, which would never be achieved in reality for either the state or its legal system.

5.4 SOCIOLOGY OF LAW

5.4.1 Objectives of sociological study

1. Sociology is the scientific study of human behaviour, especially with regard to analysis of its:
   - origins;
   - organisation;
   - institutions;
   - development of human society.
2. Such study may address general areas of academic knowledge, e.g.:
   - economics;
   - politics;
   - law.
3. More particularly, thereafter, the study may focus on specific problems, e.g.:
   - crime;
   - child abuse;
   - divorce.
4. Although not in the past identified and named as sociology, many philosophical writers have in fact considered law in its social context, from the Greeks (Plato) through to Hobbes, Locke, Montesquieu and Rousseau.
5. In the nineteenth century, political science was sufficiently advanced to differentiate society in a broad sense from what was originally identified as the Crown and later the state, and this led to the birth of modern sociology, and hence sociology of law.
6. Writers who led in this field included:
   - August Comte (1798–1857) (see section 4.2) who was first to use the word 'sociology' in 1838, and whose purpose was to identify and explain the principle stages of human development;
   - Karl Marx (1818–83), for whom law was only one of the criteria meriting consideration in achieving what he

thought to be more important historical, economic and
political objectives;

- Emile Durkheim (1858–1917), who was instrumental in
  using the scientific methodology of gathering empirical
  statistical material evidence to provide evidence on
  which to base his study of society;
- Max Weber (1864–1920), who considered a variety of
  theoretical aspects of social organisation.

7. One of the writers most directly concerned with sociological
law was Roscoe Pound, considered next.

5.4.2 Pound

1. Legal philosophy has been addressed from a variety of
traditional viewpoints, and social science has provided some
useful examples, particularly sociology and economics.

2. Roscoe Pound (1870–1964) dealt with the methodology in
Social Control Through Law (1942), categorising law and
treating it as the prime means of achieving social control
within society, as opposed to grounding it in natural law,
religious or more general moral criteria.

3. This reflects previous writings from the early decades of the
twentieth century, such as *Law and Liberty* (1914), where he
identified a new understanding of the social-philosophical
school, arguing that:

- previous dominance of self-assertion no longer prevailed;
- future juristic policy would be founded on the need to
  secure claims of society at large, i.e. social and public
  claims.

4. He brings together the different meanings of law, substance
and method into a regulatory regime based on principles
and process.

5. Sociology of law tries as far as possible to apply a scientific
methodology to its treatment of legal investigation.

6. The relatively clear criteria that underscore the legitimacy of
legal positivism, such as Austin's command theory of

sovereignty or Hart's rules, are not so easy to pinpoint in sociology of law, but tend to comprise a mixture including the:

- simple existence of society;
- habit of obedience of the population;
- political criteria present, which are to a lesser or greater extent generally accepted;
- somewhat obscure ultimate justification, which does not need in sociological terms to be pinned down.

7. According to Pound a legal system achieves legal order by:
- recognising interests such as efficiency in ordering conduct and relations;
- defining the limitations of such interests;
- recognising and giving effect to them *via* legal precepts applied by the judiciary;
- keeping them all within recognised and defined limits.

8. This presupposes three types of interest, which are treated as social rights rather than God-given or fundamental legal rights:
- individual;
- public;
- social.

9. Summarising, therefore, sociology of law is based on the propositions that:
- law is derived from the life of the community as a whole;
- it must therefore serve the interests of the generality rather than of the individual;
- it should not be a static body of knowledge, but a living, growing entity.

CHAPTER 6

MOSTLY AMERICAN

Common Law Tradition

FORMALISM
- Langdell
- Ames

PRAGMATISM
- James
- Dewey

REALISM
- Holmes
- Llewellyn
- Frank

6.1 FORMALISM

6.1.1 Langdell

1. Christopher Columbus Langdell (1826–1906) was initially a law practitioner and later appointed as first Dean of the Harvard Law School.
2. He was the author of the first student casebook selection of *Cases on the Law of Contracts* (1870), the main bases of his approach to the theory of law teaching being that:
   - law should be accorded the same approach and have a similar status to science (bearing in mind the importance of science in the nineteenth century), the law library becoming the law student's laboratory;
   - the purpose of studying legal theory is to identify the basic organising structure of the law, whether conceptually or in the form of principles;
   - the case study method of law teaching and learning was more useful than reading numerous cases or compiling notes of rules from lectures and text books, but case studies were combined with the question and answer Socratic teaching method, rigorously applied to ensure adequate student preparation;
   - legal principles could be derived from concentrated attention to relevant appellate case law, the equivalent of studying scientific specimens in the laboratory.

6.1.2 Ames

1. James Barr Ames (1846–1910) followed Langdell as Dean of Harvard Law School in 1895 and further developed the American case study method, which replaced the previous American Columbia University (Professor) Dwight method, which had entailed a combination of:
   - lecture;
   - recitation;
   - drill.

2. That system was supplemented by students reading texts followed by oral testing for memory in class.

3. Case methodology has expanded from its 1870 introduction in law studies and is now used in other fields such as business and medicine:

   - it involves reading the original (case) source materials (for law) and extracting conclusions from them;
   - by this approach students master legal principles and doctrines, the important point being that students who are going to practise law need to learn diagnosis, decision-making and judgement to put themselves in a position to be able to implement consequential practical action.

4. Formalism was an important and perhaps dominant legal study methodology in the late nineteenth and early twentieth centuries, although other influences such as realism came into fashion at about the same time or shortly thereafter.

5. The formalist methodology was a kind of inductive empiricism, knowledge and understanding being learnt by detailed study of original sources, developing the ability to apply that knowledge in a practical way, and in its contemporary form remains the dominant American approach to legal learning;

6. Modern versions emphasise difficult and contradictory cases, which might appear to contradict aspects of Langdell's theory, but the essential methodology remains the same, the current view being not that conflicting decisions were wrongly decided, but that conflicting decisions require more concentrated analysis.

6.2 PRAGMATISM

1. The American pragmatism of William James (1842–1910) and John Dewey (1859–1952) fed into American realism.

2. Pragmatism means that:
- theory needs practice to be meaningful, i.e. what is useful is what works best;
- students need to study law in a form that is real and has meaning;
- the consequences determine the practicality of what needs to be studied and applied, i.e. theory needs an operational import.

3. Another way of explaining pragmatism is to say that:
- legal norms of behaviour are sufficient in themselves to justify the law;
- this contrasts with natural law, which requires *a priori* justification.

4. Possible bases to these justifications could be:
- inductive criteria arising from the facts of cases that then influence legal precedent;
- judicial precedent based on the factual decisions that form the basis of legal realism;
- sociological conclusions that can be drawn from a study of courts and judicial practice.

6.3 REALISM

6.3.1 Basic ideas

1. Legal realism, taking these pragmatic ideas on board, challenged a number of previously held beliefs of American common law, including the ability of ordinary people to choose the laws by which they would be governed.

2. Legal realists wanted to replace the existing system of classical legal thought in the United States, which was also known by other descriptions such as formalism and mechanical jurisprudence, the general thrust of which had been to give power to business corporations at the expense of workers and consumers.

3. There were several things that had to be addressed in order to clear the ground and apply the realistic approach:
   - removal of muddled ideas that grew out of natural law theory (for example, the 'right to life or liberty' is readily sacrificed by states the moment their higher interests come into question, as by threats of terrorism or war);
   - making a clear distinction between law and morality (in researching legal problems the likely result is what is being sought, not the rights or wrongs attributable to the consequences);
   - understanding the relationship of law and logic (Holmes saying in *The Common Law* that the life of the law has not been logic, but has been made and influenced by current morals, politics and public policy).

4. Some of the characteristics of legal realism include:
   - a need for legal language to be clear and unambiguous;
   - the necessity for social reform;
   - distrust of rules;
   - concern with the psychological and ideological motivations of judges;
   - preoccupation with the validity and methodology of judicial process;
   - the idea that law is the prophecy of what the courts will do in fact rather than a consideration of naturalist concerns with principles and morality, i.e. realism means practical predictive jurisprudence.

5. It therefore involves acceptance of several fundamental notions as to the nature of law, i.e. that it is:
   - indeterminate in the sense that it is the judge rather than the content of statute or precedent that leads directly to legal outcomes;
   - interdisciplinary, as realists argue that other elements or disciplines need to be drawn into the practice of law, such as sociology (Pound) or psychology (Frank);
   - instrumental because it should be used as a means of attaining social purposes and achieving social engineering.

6.3.2 Relationship to other theories

1. Legal realism involves empirical process rather than conceptual analysis, reaction to legal formalism or mechanical jurisprudence.
2. By 'empirical' is meant that realists seek to describe how judges actually decide cases, as opposed to attempting to construct a theoretical conceptual framework of how the law might be construed.
3. This means that legal realism attributes to judges a more important law-making role than previously acknowledged, using moral and political criteria rather than applying fixed legal rules.
4. Legal realism thus by implication denies some of the previously held beliefs both of natural law and legal positivism.
5. The local indeterminacy thesis is the proposition that for appellate decisions to be reached there is often insufficient existing law available.
6. The discretion thesis allows judges to make new law when adjudicating upon cases, the ruling factor in reaching such decisions being political and moral opinion more than law (but with the whole process resulting in new law).
7. Realism relies on and does not contradict legal positivism, but places emphasis on the social and psychological attitudes of the judiciary.

6.3.3 Holmes

1. Oliver Wendell Holmes (1841–1935) explains American legal realism or predictive jurisprudence in *The Common Law* (1881), and exemplifies this in his *Harvard Law Review* article 'The Path of Law' (1897) 'bad man' thesis where:
   - the bad man does not care two straws for axioms (self-evident admitted principles) or deductions;
   - the objective of law study is to predict outcomes in order to advise clients;

- statutes, case reports and treatises are the 'oracles' through which this is effected;
- the process is by 'prophecy' of outcomes;
- the bad man thesis is used to differentiate morality from laws, the bad man's main concern being to avoid penalties and punishments such as fines or imprisonment, rather than worrying himself about societal consequences;
- it is a fallacy to assume that only logic propels development of the law;
- the previous important role of history in legal interpretation needed to be reduced.

2. Holmes emphasised (and was able to implement practically as he was an American Supreme Court Justice from 1902 to 1932) that:
   - experience rather than logic was often what drove developments in the law;
   - working out what the courts would in fact do in particular cases was what comprised the real purpose of law;
   - the historical origins of the law were not of much contemporary assistance in this endeavour.

3. He insisted on the rejection of what he saw as Man's search for the superlative, which was the basis of belief in natural law, thus creating a clear distinction between law and morality.

4. It might be argued that at its simplest the beliefs and objectives of pragmatism and realism are self-evident, but there are some valid criticisms to be made:
   - predictions are not the same thing as rules;
   - any tendency to remove morality from legal implementation is dangerous and to many if not most people unsatisfactory and unacceptable;
   - carried to extremes, strict adherence to realist ideas means that the search for wider truths is abandoned, and a series of dimensions lost to jurisprudence.

5. A contemporary of Holmes was John Chipman Gray (1839–1915), who argued that statutes were legal sources but that the law itself consisted of the actual decisions of courts, i.e. the rules laid down by judges.

6.3.4 Llewellyn

1. Karl Nickerson Llewellyn (1893–1962) published *The Bramble Bush* in 1930, having studied law at Yale, but played a role of bringing in continental European influence to American legal theory:

- he fought for the Germans in the First World War, winning the Iron Cross;
- after qualifying he was instrumental in developing American realism at Columbia, his legal realism being influenced by the German 'free law' movement;
- realism provides the *post-hoc* (after the event) rationalisation for legal decisions made by judges on whatever their theoretical reasoning might have been;
- law is 'indeterminate', i.e. in reaching a novel decision the existing law could not provide a justification or explanation;
- in practice it means that a judge usually has the discretion or ability to distinguish previous decisions, or to apply them in the instant case, in either case by using legitimate arguments and reasons;

2. Llewellyn took the 'sociological' line in emphasising the social forces that acted upon judges in reaching their decisions (as opposed to the 'idiosyncratic' tendency represented by Frank).

3. He was involved in the drafting of the Uniform Commercial Code in the 1940s, incorporating a pervading aura of good faith that would enable the judge to reach what he considered to be his own common-sense adjudication;

4. Reflecting Holmes and Gray, Llewellyn believed that law was what officials (i.e. all those involved in the administration of the law, especially but not exclusively judges) actually do when citizens are involved in disputes:

- this meant that by understanding the way that officials used the rules, and immersing oneself in the style and methodology of appellate courts, it was possible to predict the results of most cases;
- such an approach was more appropriate, effective and nearer to reaching the kernel of the nature of law than any study of textbooks and principles was likely to be.

6.3.5 Frank

1. Jerome Frank (1889–1957) was critical of other realists, himself being prepared in some ways to go further than the others:
   - his assumptions were that the obvious and apparent purpose of law is to settle disputes, which cannot be done by believing that it is rules of law which determine how decisions are going to be reached;
   - he called himself a 'fact-sceptic' whilst others were only 'rule-sceptics';
   - such others had a bias towards appellate courts, whereas it was the infinitely variable facts that could be found in the lower courts that determined the vast majority of cases;
   - it followed that fundamentally it was the attitudes of the lower judges, juries, parties and witnesses that decided cases;
   - the law only came into existence on the point or case in question when the judge had made his decision.
2. Frank was interested in psychological aspects of legal practice, believing that knowledge of the human condition in the sense of the background and consequential prejudices and biases of the judge was vital to win cases.
3. There are several suppositions or questions that arise:
   - how far is it really true to say that the law is created by judges, as opposed to legislation being interpreted by them?

- is it correct that judges often start from the position of having reached a decision on the case being tried, and then working backwards?
- if this view of realism is true, does it follow that rights and obligations are decided retrospectively, thus producing result-oriented jurisprudence?

4. This gives rise to additional and more specific questions of whether there can be any place in a legal system, given such beliefs, for:
- ideals;
- justice;
- morality;
- fairness.

6.3.6 Scandinavian realists

1. Scandinavian realists take a different stance to that of the Americans, arguing that the key to how the law works is to examine the psychological reaction of legal arguments on the minds of officials and other caught up in the law's administration.

2. Axel Hagerstrom (1868–1939), a Swedish academic, was responsible for the origins of this and he strongly criticised theories of law that referred to moral content:
- modern law worked on the basis of what people still believed after the magic or mysticism of the beliefs of earlier generations had faded;
- those who asserted rights exuded power, whilst those who believed they had obligations tended to be subjugated.

3. Karl Olivecrona (1897–1980), also Swedish, developed these lines of argument using Hagerstrom's approach:
- he dismissed the command theory and the use of abstractions to explain the law;
- the actual provisions of the law as found in statutes and formal sources were not important, rather the effect they had on people's minds was what mattered;

- law was the accumulated weight of ideas that permeated the current mass psyche, turned into orders *via* the current law, and recorded in the formal documentation of the system;
- any wish to disobey will eventually be overcome in order to achieve peace of mind, and so norms of behaviour are established;
- he is criticised on the basis that his ideas are theoretical and rely on the use of language, rather than being based on actual investigation of how the law operates on a daily and practical basis.

4. Alf Ross (1899–1979) was a Danish Scandinavian realist, despite his name, and his writings sought to address some of the criticisms made of the psychological approach to understanding law:
   - he proposed a species of logical positivism;
   - this meant that explanations of the law could only be meaningful if they could be verified objectively, so they could be used (as in practical American realism) to predict the behaviour of officials.

6.4 CRITICAL LEGAL STUDIES

6.4.1 Scope

1. In a broad context critical legal theory can be traced back as far as the origins of natural law, in that many generations of scholars have sought to challenge the wisdom of their predecessors.
2. In a narrow and the usual modern sense, critical legal studies grew out of realism roots into a critique of existing attitudes within the mainly American common law system, expanding the indeterminacy thesis into other fields.
3. The modern movement originates from the 1960s although it was only formally recognised in the late 1970s.

4. Influenced by a variety of earlier European writers such as Marx and Engels, Weber and Marcuse, Gramsci, Foucault and Derrida, the focus is on:
   - showing that law justifies and reinforces those who wield power in society;
   - consideration of the nature and extent of injustices, how they managed to become legitimated in the first place, and how once that has happened the position might be rectified;
   - emphasising the political purposes served by law and the legal system;
   - using other social science theory (e.g. economics and political philosophy) to reinforce its claims;

5. It has grown out of legal realism and has either formed the subject-matter of or influenced other recent legal theory such as:
   - feminism;
   - critical race theory;
   - postmodernism, influenced by literary theory;
   - some aspects of economic law theory;

6. It may:
   - be referred to by other descriptions, such as 'outsider jurisprudence';
   - often better be characterised by differences between writers than similarities or consistency, even within the same subject areas;
   - encompass other elements of modernity such as globalisation and questions about the current or new world order in which we live.

7. Examples of the varied writers within the broad band of critical legal studies include:
   - Robert W Gordon;
   - Morton J Horwitz;
   - Duncan Kennedy;
   - Catharine A MacKinnon;
   - Roberto Mangabeira Unger.

6.4.2 Feminism

1. Feminism in its contemporary form refers to the relatively modern stage of the feminist political movement, sometimes described in terms of waves (perhaps reflecting the three generational 'liberty, equality and fraternity' theory of human rights), the sequence comprising and incorporating:
   - first wave claims for universal suffrage starting in the late nineteenth century;
   - second wave claims for equality in education, work and in marital relationships;
   - third wave claims in other spheres including race, ethnicity, class, nationality, politics and religion.

2. This is a limited political perspective, however, as throughout history women have in different contexts argued for and in some cases been able to obtain and practise equality or superiority.

3. It might be described as an approach to the study of legal theory that takes the position of women as its starting point and objective, in which case the contrast is going to be with the pre-existing bias in favour of male-centred viewpoints, and where there may be a tendency towards an inter-disciplinary approach

4. The women's liberation movement is a broadly liberal commitment to and advocacy for increased women's freedoms, and so is linked to the wider rights movement.

5. A further classification can be made between a descriptive fact or normative claim approach, an instance of the *is* and the *ought*, where it is argued that women are disadvantaged in various ways (e.g. by not having equal pay, despite legislation to that end), but that they ought not to be discriminated against.

6. There are various views within feminism as to what constitutes inequality, what are its causes, and a particular question sometimes posed is whether existing accounts of law, morality and justice are adequate, or require a specifically revised feminist agenda.

7. The difficulty of categorising the phenomenon because of the complexity of issues and differing types of injustice has led to other terms being used on occasion, including womanism and intersectionality.

8. 'Womanism' is a term that was used as far back as the 1860s, and intersectionality involves problems arising from apparent combinations of discrimination such as using violence against women for more than one reason, e.g. as intimidation and as a political weapon.

9. There is no one universal cause of inequality between women and men, and causative factors will differ from one society to another, e.g. arising from educational, general economic or specific work-based causes, religion, sexual objectification and for many other reasons.

10. From a consideration of such factors it will be seen that there is no single agreed definition of 'feminism', but there are many different kinds and approaches to the subject, so care should be taken whenever considering the topic carefully to define the scope and extent of the discussion.

6.4.3 Race and law

1. The basic thesis of critical race theory is that racial minorities have always been disadvantaged and even with the abolition of slavery and enactment of more recent anti-discriminatory laws, legal disadvantages, and their practical knock-on effects and consequences, remain.

2. Discussion mostly originates and takes place mainly in the United States, although the issues are relevant in most jurisdictions including the United Kingdom.

3. The following are examples of the kinds of question that can be framed to address the issues covered by the race and law thesis:
   - how far does the legal system (substantively and instrumentally) reflect and serve the interests of those who control state apparatus (i.e. the establishment or other ruling cliques) at the expense of the relatively disenfranchised racial minorities?

- to what extent do particular legal devices or activities (statutes, ways of choosing the judiciary, police methods etc.) really take into consideration the circumstances and needs of racial minorities (e.g. 'stop and search' policies)?
- to what extent are historical wrongs perpetrated on peoples (aborigines, Maoris, native North Americans etc.) the responsibility of present generations (the reparations debate)?
- how can we judge whether the current domestic legal regime fairly addresses racial issues, and on the basis that there is still much injustice, what should be done about it?

6.4.4 Postmodernism

1. This is a complex issue and difficult to pin down, because it has a wide-ranging set of meanings crossing boundaries of culture, history, art, literature, philosophy, law and other areas.
2. The more immediately relevant considerations here are:
   - history;
   - philosophy;
   - law.
3. Characteristics of postmodernism in history include:
   - a movement towards having less confidence in progress;
   - disappointment with political failure.
4. In philosophy, it involves scepticism about such matters as:
   - certainty of achieving understanding about the nature and extent of knowledge;
   - how language is used to construct rather than reflect reality.
5. For law, factors to be considered are that:
   - there is no natural law on which an overarching theoretical construct can be hung;
   - neither can there be anything approaching a perfect legally posited system, e.g. by formulating a constitution or regime of rights;

- there can therefore not be 'a' or 'the' right way of interpreting law.
6. The nearest one can get to the ideal is to balance laws, rules and principles one against the other, against a continuously moving and developing background.

JURAL OPPOSITES	
Right	No right
Privilege	Duty
Power	Disability
Immunity	Liability

JURAL CORRELATIVES	
Right	Duty
Privilege	No right
Power	Liability
Immunity	Disability

INTRODUCTION

The subject matter of this chapter is described as contemporary theory for the following reasons:

- Hohfeld, although writing in the early twentieth century, had significant influence on understanding and development of the character of human rights and obligations;
- Hart carried forward into the modern age the legal positivism of Austin, but giving it real current relevance, for example by his work on rules and by the content and breadth of his various debates;
- Dworkin is certainly contemporary, and his work has gone some way to reconcile traditional strands of jurisprudential thought;
- Theories of justice discussed by Rawls and entitlement by Nozick lie at the heart of much of today's legal philosophical debate, and call for continuing attention by modern scholars;
- Law and economics cannot be ignored in the twenty-first century, when capitalism and globalisation seem set to dictate much of what is likely to happen in the foreseeable future;
- Other writers or themes could have been selected, but these give something of contemporary flavour and all continue strands of legal theory dealt with in previous chapters.

7.1 HOHFELD

1. Wesley Newcombe Hohfeld (1879–1917) attempted to strip down and define basic legal concepts to enable them to be discussed and explained unambiguously, utilising analytical as opposed to normative jurisprudence, which he set out in *Fundamental Legal Conceptions as Applied in Judicial Reasoning* (published after his death in 1919).

2. He did this by expanding on the basic simple assumption that rights and duties are opposite sides of the same coin, using the concept of fundamental jural relations, which he elaborated as jural opposites and jural correlatives.

3. Jural opposites are:
   - right – no-right;
   - privilege – duty;
   - power – disability;
   - immunity – liability.

4. Jural opposites arise where, if one of the factors under consideration applies to a person, he cannot at the same time be under a disability posed by the opposite, e.g.:
   - if X has the power to alter a legal relationship, he cannot at the same time be subject to any disability that prevents him from so doing;
   - if Y has an immunity against Z, there can be no simultaneous liability to Z on the same subject.

5. Jural correlatives are:
   - right – duty;
   - privilege – no-right;
   - power – liability;
   - immunity – disability.

6. Jural correlatives must exist in conjunction with each other, so if one person has the benefit of immunity in a particular context, the other person must be subject to a disability.

7. Instead of restricting himself to the use of the word 'right' as a blanket description for the relationship of 'something' asserted by a person X in respect of something Y to be desired, Hohfeld refined the meaning of the word into four strictly fundamental legal relations:
   - right (or claim), as where a landlord has the right to claim rent due to him by a tenant;
   - privilege, which comprises a person's freedom to do or refrain from doing some action;
   - power (which is more than a mere privilege), e.g. where a person has the freedom to choose to do something that

changes other persons' legal rights and duties, such as being able to dispose of property;

- immunity, where a person has no legal power to alter existing legal relations with another person.

8. This multiple juxtaposition of terms that had previously often been used loosely and indiscriminately means that:

- all relationships between X and Y can be brought within the jural framework and categorised as either right, privilege, power or immunity, each having distinctive characteristics *vis-à-vis* the other;
- these relationships can be demonstrated diagrammatically and geometrically;
- a much higher (though still not schematically perfect) degree of precision can be brought to bear on jural relationships.

9. Hohfeld's analysis was timely, providing as it did in the early twentieth century a theoretical framework and rigorous calculus for the developing notion of human rights that, following the Second World War, went a long way towards both continuing and replacing the natural rights tradition.

10. Influenced by him, the modern rights tradition has grown into sets of global, regional and national norms that are followed, or used as a stick to beat those who fail to follow, what are claimed to be universal standards.

7.2 HART

7.2.1 *The Concept of Law*

1. HLA Hart (1907–92) addresses deficiencies in legal positivism that he sees (amongst others) in the approaches of his predecessors Bentham, and Austin, and his contemporary Kelsen.

2. In *The Concept of Law* (1961) he puts forward ideas that attempt to provide a more complete answer to the question

of what constitutes law, going beyond the narrow command and purity interpretations and restrictions imposed on themselves by Austin and Kelsen respectively.

3. If legal philosophers consciously confine their discussion to particular considerations such as sovereignty, sanctions or morality, they are not going to be able to explain law with universal values in relation to what Hart sees as the different rules that make up its constituent parts.

4. He is also concerned with:
   - the nature of language;
   - how its use affects understanding of law.

5. In dealing with the law it is impossible to take everything into consideration, which limits the ability of legal philosophers to address the constantly arising new situations that operating the legal system entails.

6. The previous emphasis on the command theory of law, by which it is argued that the legal system forces people into obedience by sanctions, is:
   - correct in some particulars and so far as it goes;
   - incomplete, as many citizens obey law not out of fear but out of a sense of obligation to do what they consider to be right;
   - and what that is perceived to be will vary from one time and place to another.

7. So there are internal and external influences that are brought to bear:
   - externally the citizen is obliged, by orders or commands reinforced by fear of sanctions, to be obedient;
   - internally the citizen may be regarded as being under an obligation to obey legal rules setting acceptable standards because compliance is accepted by him under a sense of duty, rather than being imposed upon him from above by a political sovereign (body).

8. The internal element is Hart's development of the concept of law:
   - beyond Austin's sanctions and commands theory and Kelsen's clinical skeletal theoretical analysis;

- which advances to one that posits *rules* as a means of amplifying existing theories into a more cohesive and comprehensive whole that could also (like Kelsen) be applied on a wider basis than simply one given legal system.

9. Hart does not restrict himself in this way but explains the operation of law in a wider context by looking at the nature of the rules that are always and universally likely to apply.

7.2.2 Primary and secondary rules

1. This is achieved by developing a theory of the union of primary and secondary rules, which has a number of characteristics:
   - analytical;
   - positivist;
   - sociological, to an extent.
2. Primary rules:
   - impose duties, setting out what people should or should not do;
   - comprise specific categories of law, such as the rules governing contract, tort or crime.
3. Secondary rules are of three types, being in effect rules about rules, concerned with what primary rules allow or prevent individuals from doing, and comprising:
   - rules of recognition;
   - rules of adjudication;
   - rules of change.

7.2.3 Rules of recognition

1. These confer legal validity and are used to determine the validity of primary rules, e.g.:
   - the rule that courts cannot challenge the validity of statutes (see, e.g. *British Railways Board v Pickin* [1974] AC 765);

- this approach would perhaps require further consideration in light of current European Union law, e.g. the fisheries litigation (see *Factortame Ltd v Secretary of State for Transport (No. 2)* [1991] 1 All ER 70).

2. The secondary rule of recognition is the fundamental rule justifying the validity of the legal system, so in the United Kingdom it would be the rule that establishes that legislation is valid if it is made by the properly constituted parliamentary procedure and confirmed by the Crown (cf. Kelsen's *grundnorm*, see section 4.5.2).

3. These in themselves are not always adequate explanation, however, as there are other recognised ways of making law, e.g.
   - subordinate legislation;
   - custom, in limited circumstances;
   - judicial precedent.

4. They are rules about rules, concerned with what primary rules allow or prevent individuals from doing.

7.2.4 Rules of adjudication

1. These confer power, and allow us to determine whether a primary rule has been broken, such rules being either procedural or remedial in nature.

2. Rules of adjudication are those that provide judicial authority to determine disputes, such as the rules of court.

3. Examining legal systems in the light of this union of primary and secondary rules enables students to go beyond the restrictive visions provided by previous writers more broadly to explain the nature of law as it now operates.

7.2.5 Rules of change

1. These confer power, allowing an individual or institution to change primary rules, e.g. the rule that Parliament can change the law through the process of legislation.

2. Rules of change may be private or public:
- private rules of change alter relationships between individuals, e.g. the rules of contract that deal with powers rather than duties of individuals;
- public rules of change also give power, but in this case to public officials to make, vary or amend primary rules as changing circumstances of society might require.

3. Public officials are those people charged with the making and administration of rules, e.g. legislators and judiciary, not limited to the more usual meaning implying (say) civil servants or local government officers.

4. Secondary rules are therefore supportive of primary rules, influencing the ways in which violation of primary rules can be rectified.

5. The system only works, however, when there is a *union* of primary and secondary rules.

7.2.6 Implications and criticisms

1. The officials who administer the rules comprise:
- legislators;
- judges;
- administrators.

2. These officials must have an 'inner view' of the secondary rules, i.e. a conscious desire to comply with them and accept them as valid, in addition to (but also separate from) any Austinian insistence on sovereignty and sanctions.

3. The inner view is Hart's explanation of Kelsen's *grundnorm*.

4. In order to avoid the criticism that positivism lends support to morally dubious systems of law, Hart also insists that some facts relating to the human condition require all valid systems of law to observe certain universal factors to be designated as such.

5. Examples that illustrate the kinds of fact to be considered are that:
- not all humans are of equal physical strength, or have comparable economic or social power;

- there do not exist infinite resources to supply people's needs;
- knowledge is unequally distributed amongst the population.

6. In considering the separation of law and morals as it relates to legal positivism, Hart identifies three components of utilitarian jurisprudence, namely that:
    - it is necessary to separate law and morals;
    - there is a need to undertake an analytical study of legal phenomena;
    - law exists and should be construed as a command.

7. But he goes on to say that law is more than mere command theory because:
    - it is wrong to think of a legislature with a periodically changing membership as a group of persons habitually obeyed;
    - such an idea only applies to a long surviving monarch ('long-surviving' because it was always a weakness of Austinian legal positivism that a monarch new to the throne, or to power depending on the terms of discussion, by that fact alone could not previously have enjoyed and exerted habitual obedience);
    - legislatures make law not because they have the power to enforce rules, but because they comply with fundamental rules defining the law-making process;
    - not all laws take the form of commands, some (and indeed many, especially non-criminal laws) conferring rights rather than duties.

8. Criticisms of Hart's rules-based theory include the following:
    - his claim that all societies must recognise certain basic assumptions about the human condition ignores the fact that the value placed on various actions differs drastically from one society to another, e.g. compare conditions in Myanmar, the Sudan and the United Kingdom;
    - as an example, it is acceptable under some legal systems to punish criminals by amputating the limbs of thieves,

and under others to hold convicted (even mentally ill) prisoners for decades before executing them;

- the concept of equality is incapable of being given a universally acceptable definition, and in some societies it is not understood, wanted or acceptable;
- the relationship between law, morality and justice remains problematical, and is also subject to culturally relative interpretation;
- it is over-simplistic to classify legal rules as merely either imposing duties or conferring powers;
- on occasion principles may have to outweigh rules, e.g. to prevent a son benefiting by inheritance from the murder of his parent;
- loyalty to rules is an over-simplification of why officials do their duty;
- the role of legal institutions with regard to the legal system also remains problematical.

7.3 DWORKIN

7.3.1 The third way

1. Ronald Dworkin (b. 1931) takes what is sometimes described as a third way or position between natural law and legal positivism, his response in *Law's Empire* to Hart's version of positivism.
2. He does not accept natural law notions of pervading moral norms required to shape the law and that expect law to be analogous to justice, although he does accept that moral principles are relevant to law when they are actually applied by judges.
3. Whilst accepting that there are legal rules to guide behaviour, he nevertheless rejects those premises of legal positivism that limit judgements of what law is about and that require complete separation of law and morality.

4. Austin's sanctions, Kelsen's norms and Hart's rules of recognition are all substantial but only partial approaches to understanding what can be considered as law.

5. In order fully to appreciate the essential nature of law there is a need to go beyond Hart's rules and consider policies and principles as well.

6. Rules and principles differ:
   - rules either apply to a particular situation or they don't;
   - principles are broader and more flexible;
   - these are tools that allow the right conclusion to be reached even in uncertain situations where an obvious answer is not apparent.

7. Conflicting principles have to be weighed one against another to determine in particular circumstances which of them should prevail.

8. Hence the rule of law that would allow a son to inherit from his parent, even if he had murdered that parent, which has to be overborne by the overriding principle that prevents criminals benefiting from their crimes.

9. Dworkin's writings can be recognised as having three phases:
   - initially he addressed Hart's contention that law comprises a set of rules which judges can use to reach decisions, but ignoring matters such as policies and principles that were not rule-based;
   - he made further inroads into legal positivism by inventing a device in the form of the all-knowing judge, Hercules, to deal with hard cases, and who is able to reach the just and right judgment however difficult the case or obscure the underlying law;
   - in *Law's Empire* and later work the notion of constructive interpretation is developed, the interpretivist theory being that legal rights and duties are determined by a community's best interpretation of political practice, which has two aspects:
     - the reading of a legal text must achieve a 'fit' criterion;
     - where more than one interpretation is fit, it is the best one that must be applied to optimise the community's political practices.

7.3.2 Policies, principles and trumps

1. As indicated above, Dworkin goes beyond early ideas of command (Austin) and later rule-based positivism (Hart) to a consideration of principles and policies:
   - principles means observable standards whose purpose is to further some abstract quality of justice, fairness, equity or morality;
   - policies are more specific and particular objectives or standards limited to political, social or economic aims;
2. The ordinary meaning of the words should be borne in mind to explain the distinction:
   - policies are more restricted, immediate, worldly;
   - principles are in contrast more high-minded, moral, incorporating qualities to which a valid legal system needs to aspire.
3. Rights manifested in the form of principles will always be 'trumps', more important than and overruling policies where there is conflict between them:
   - they cannot normally be sacrificed, although sometimes policies must be;
   - strong rights can never be negated;
   - nevertheless, in the nature of things and recognising realities, weaker rights may sometimes need to be equated with policies, if there is a really substantial greater goal represented by a policy, but this must be the exceptional case.

7.3.3 The role of the judge

1. Dworkin bases some of his legal philosophy on the process judges use to decide cases (thus inviting comparison with American realists):
   - judges should adjudicate by applying to hard cases the best justification from the principles of political morality that they can find;
   - the hypothetical judge Hercules, when faced with hard

cases, has superhuman perception in order to compare with and contrast the human frailties of the real judiciary (thus correcting the weak humanity of realist judges, whose decisions might depend on out of which side of bed they had climbed that morning, or what they had eaten for breakfast);

- Hercules produces irrefutable arguments in all circumstances to demonstrate what the law is, and that there is only one right answer to every legal problem;

- real judges, however, can only confront a limited portion of the total system, with restricted knowledge of the circumstances and incomplete understanding that they can bring to bear, whereas the all-seeing Hercules addresses the theoretical whole.

7.3.4 The chain novel

1. One illustration that Dworkin uses to demonstrate his thinking is a theoretical chain novel symbolic of the linked growth of law, which can be used to illustrate the process by which the law gradually develops, with many authors (judges) over time adding chapters to the plot (binding precedents for the common law):

- a group of novelists are employed to write one novel (e.g. the law of contract, or perhaps more specifically the law of consideration or contractual capacity);

- they draw numbered lots and the one with the lowest number writes the first chapter;

- number 2 has to write chapter 2 by interpreting chapter 1, the purpose being to produce the best possible end result;

- all subsequent writers must give direction to and expand the work in progress, and all are capable of influencing to a lesser or greater extent the overall direction the novel (law) will take;

- they are not able or allowed to write a series of short stories, because that would negate the principle of development involved in judicial precedent and prevent

the proper operation of the court hierarchy;
- instead, they must strive to achieve a coherent whole by continuing the flow from the past through the instant case to provide a valid precedent for the future.

2. Translated to the legal system, this means that a judge with a natural law tendency may be unable to reach his own ideal decision because of the precedents by which he is bound, influenced by the following criteria:
  - Dworkin distinguishes internal and external scepticism:
    - the former does not challenge the idea that good arguments can be found in principle for one interpretation rather than another;
    - the latter does not deny that one interpretation of the legal record can be objectively characterised as the correct interpretation;
  - however, he rejects the notion that external scepticism justifies the argument that morality has nothing to do with legal theory, thus leaving the naturalism door partially open in posited legal systems;
  - so when cases come to court there must be a recognition that the outcome is never certain because litigants have rights that go beyond narrow and generally accepted boundaries, albeit to some extent restricted by proper interpretation of the common standard of the political order;
  - this leads to surprising results, disappointment, despair and sometimes injustice, but is better than the alternatives that might apply, according to Dworkin.

7.4 JUSTICE

7.4.1 Justice as fairness

1. John Rawls (b. 1921):
   - established his ideas in a paper called 'Justice as Fairness' in the *Philosophical Review* in 1958;

- developed them in a series of subsequent papers and articles;
- brought them together in his book *A Theory of Justice* (1971, revised 1999);
- restated them in *Political Liberalism* (1993).

2. The structure of the revised edition of *A Theory of Justice* deals with theory in the first part, institutions in the second, and ends of justice in part three.

3. His central aims and ideas formed the basis for a constitutional democracy, as an alternative to the utilitarianism pervading the Anglo-Saxon legal tradition (see chapter 5), because the greatest good may not always produce the desired effect for a variety of reasons:
   - unfairness arises when the increased happiness of group A leads to the decreased happiness of group B;
   - legal philosophy taking the natural law approach should be able to produce theory which overcomes that kind if inequity.

4. Justice as fairness is a theoretical social contractarian and libertarian approach and relies on two principles of *fair equality of opportunity* and the *difference principle*:
   - the first statement of the two principles says that each person is to have an equal right to the most extensive scheme of equal basic liberties compatible with a similar scheme of liberties for others;
   - the second principle states that social and economic inequalities are to be arranged so that they are both:
     - to the greatest benefit of the least advantaged, consistent with the savings principle, and;
     - attached to offices and positions open to all under the conditions of fair equality of opportunity.

7.4.2 Priority rules and distribution

1. It is necessary to apply Rawls' first and second principles in conjunction with his two priority rules, *The Priority of Liberty* and *The Priority of Justice over Efficiency and Welfare*.

2. Under the first priority rule justice principles are ranked in lexical order (i.e. the order which requires us to satisfy the first principle before moving on to the second and third etc.) so that:
   - reducing liberty can only be done if the result is to increase everyone's liberty;
   - decreasing equal liberty can only be done if people with less liberty are prepared to accept it.
3. Under the second priority rule:
   - the principle of justice is prior to that of efficiency;
   - fair opportunity comes before the difference principle;
   - inequality of opportunity is allowable only if it increases the opportunities of people with less opportunity;
   - overall excessive saving rates must mitigate on balance the burden of those who have to bear that hardship.
4. Distribution of all social primary goods must be equal unless advantage would accrue to the worst off people by unequal distribution.
5. His notion of lexical distribution means that even if a suggested system of distribution is more economically efficient than another, it cannot be utilised if it would result in injustice to some of the potential recipients.

7.4.3 Original position

1. Rawls suggests an 'original position' under which there would exist a 'veil of ignorance', an ideal theoretical system where justice principles are made from scratch by moral and rational people to whom a number of considerations would apply, i.e. they:
   - do not know who they would be under the new order (e.g. their age, sex, physical strength);
   - do not know what role they would fulfil (e.g. social or economic status);
   - would not be influenced by personal motives in making decisions (whether selfish or representative of a particular interest);

- would act with the general benefit of society at heart, bearing in mind the above considerations;
- would operate under permanent rules to avoid unfair advantage subsequently accruing to one group of people at the expense of another;
- would have the same rules applied to all members of the group at all times, for the same reason.

2. Rawls believes that a social system must be designed and chosen carefully in order to ensure that distributive justice operates fairly, however things turn out, and this requires a just constitution securing:
   - liberty to enjoy equal citizenship;
   - fair equality of opportunity;
   - willingness by people to act justly although not to abandon their legitimate interests;
   - four branches of government, in order to deal with:
     - allocation;
     - stabilisation;
     - transfer;
     - distribution.

7.4.4 Operating principles

1. Perhaps somewhat surprisingly, people operating the system need not be altruistic, sacrificing themselves for the common good, because under Rawls' scheme they have to take measured decisions based on the fact that they might end up disadvantaged, and it would thus be in their interests (and everyone else's) to ensure that overall fair provision was made for everybody:
   - this is how the original position is linked to the veil of ignorance;
   - whether or not people are actually being selfish, the circumstances of justice bring about conflicting individual claims.

2. So Rawls produces three important ideas, comprising the:
   - difference principle;

- original position;
- priority of liberty.

3. The *status quo* argument, that inequality is necessary in order to provide incentives, is refuted, unless the extent of existing inequality actually manages to achieve an increase in the welfare of those disadvantaged by the inequality, i.e. the worst off, as opposed to the utilitarian average.

4. The objective is to limit the pursuit of self-interest in seeking justice and fairness in distribution of goods, a particular application of the golden rule of 'do as you would be done by'.

7.4.5 Theory of entitlement

1. Robert Nozick (b. 1938) was critical of Rawls on the grounds that he based his philosophy on what Nozick considered to be false assumptions, particularly that:
    - people want and are supposed to act for the good of everyone, and that individual assets should be available for the benefit of society;
    - redistributive approaches to goods (taking from the rich to give to the poor) are justifiable and correct;
    - government has a right to interfere with and control individual lives to carry out their political objectives;
    - Rawls' position is an 'end-state' one, whereas the better approach is to take a 'historical' position, i.e. that people have previously acquired property without reference to justice or fair principles;
    - Rawls ideology requires a pattern or plan for the provision of justice within society that does not and cannot exist.

2. Instead Nozick argues for a theory of entitlements where it is quite permissible for people to have and hold property on however an unequal basis, provided it was acquired legitimately in the first place.

3. There is never a time when everything can be collected together and a general state of equality achieved in order to

implement redistribution of assets, i.e. it is not possible to have a central distributor of goods.

4. Instead, Nozick suggests the need for three justice principles:
   - justice in acquisition, i.e. how things that were previously not owned by anyone can be acquired by an individual;
   - justice in transfer, i.e. how ownership and possession of property can subsequently be transferred from A to B;
   - justice in rectification, i.e. how injustice arising from failure fairly to apply the first two principles properly can be put right.

5. In the questions of how one should obtain, own and transfer property there are echoes of John Locke (see chapter 3), who was also interested in the ownership of things that people manufactured, and of things that previously had not belonged to anyone, provided this was done fairly.

6. In Nozick's view, however unequal ownership now is, the entitlement theory allows it to remain the same, provided acquisition and transfer came about in accordance with his first two rules.

7. Overall this is a political viewpoint that:
   - is concerned with justice, but not with Rawls' redistributive version;
   - minimises the role of the state in the lives of individuals;
   - downplays the need for and use of legal devices such as taxation, compulsory purchase, welfare provision and other coercive and compensatory devices and methods;
   - argues that unfairness cannot be avoided if private property is compulsorily acquired for public purposes, or taxation is used to enrich one group of people at the expense of others, which can be regarded as the equivalent of forced labour.

8. Nozick's ideas can be criticised on several grounds:
   - he reaches universal conclusions from individual motivations, without fully considering possible universal implications;

- he too easily reaches the point of arguing for absolute rights for freedom of action and from coercion, yet with minimum safeguards for the community;
- many people accept that benefits in favour of some people may sometimes be offset by the cost to others, despite his arguments to the contrary;
- there is not such clear-cut agreement about the nature of rights as he appears to suppose.

7.5 LAW AND ECONOMICS

7.5.1 Variety of origins

1. Libertarian approaches to jurisprudence can produce quite different theories, and legal philosophers argue that justice and other desirable legal objectives can be achieved by following different paths.
2. Law and economics, one of the more influential modern movements, nevertheless has its origins in a number of legal economist (or economic lawyer) writings, some of the main ones being:
   - Adam Smith (1723–90);
   - Jeremy Bentham (1748–1832);
   - Max Weber (1864–1920);
   - Friedrich August von Hayek (1899–1992);
   - Ronald Coase (b. 1910);
   - Bruno Leoni (1913–67);
   - Richard Posner (b. 1939).
3. One of the main strongholds of law and economics in recent decades has been the University of Chicago Law School, where both Coase and Posner exerted considerable influence.
4. Coase was the editor of *The Journal of Law and Economics* and previously made his name by applying economic principles to the operation of law in a number of ways, explaining how:

- institutions of the law have an important role to play in determining transaction costs;
- this in turn affects the allocation of economic resources;
- regulatory systems can encourage or suppress rights in property;
- transaction costs indicate why firms and businesses are organised as they are.

5. In summary, he regarded his main achievement as encouraging economists and lawyers to write about the way markets operate and how governments perform their regulatory and economic activities.

6. He was awarded a Nobel Prize and his Coase theorem says that assigning clear property rights will allow the market to reduce pollution, which formed an instrumental part of deregulatory policies in the 1980s.

7. Leoni writes about how the spontaneous historical development of the common law is being replaced by legislation, this process tending to lead to loss of individual freedom.

7.5.2 Posner

1. Economic analysis of law is the jurisprudential school that analyses legal rules and the institutions of law by reference to the methodology of microeconomics.

2. Richard Posner explains the importance and relevance of studying law and economics in several ways:
   - above all else, it is the most efficient way of explaining how legal systems actually operate, and how they ought to operate;
   - efficiency means maximising the willingness of society to pay;
   - philosophical input comes from a variety of legal backgrounds, thus ensuring common law and civil jurisdictional contributions and an international dimension, as can be seen from the above list of writers:

- Britain (Smith, Bentham, Coase, although the latter worked for much of his life in the United States);
- the US (Posner);
- Austria (Hayek);
- Italy (Leoni);
- it encourages a comparativist attitude to law study, enabling comparison of Anglo-American adversarial system with continental Europe's civil inquisitorial methodology;
- it provides a realistic forum for the study of vitally important subjects in the modern liberal globalised world, e.g.:
  - taxation and anti-trust (anti-monopoly) laws;
  - securities regulation;
  - international trade;
- other areas of economic activity that in recent years have spread to:
  - tort;
  - contract;
  - family law;
  - intellectual property law;
  - (international) criminal, and many others.

3. Posner was also appointed by President Reagan as a US Seventh Circuit Court of Appeal Judge, which enables him to apply economic legal principles to the administration of justice in a practical context, as a judicial-management tool, which he does in an assertive manner.

4. It should perhaps be mentioned that much of the literature on economics and the law is extremely technical and formulaic, and that Posner is able to bring the economic approach to law to bear on widely differing subject matter, e.g.:
   - (general) economic analysis of law;
   - the economic structure of tort law;
   - the law and economics of contract interpretation;
   - economic analysis of the use of citations in the law;
   - the economic structure of intellectual property law.

7.5.3 Practical operation

1. Economic analysis of law may perhaps be best understood by applying it to a particular subject area such as tort, the law of rectification of private wrongs done by one citizen or body against another, examples of such wrongs being:
   - negligence;
   - trespass;
   - slander;
   - nuisance etc.
2. Rectification of wrongs may be achieved in ways based on differing principles, e.g.:
   - compensation for the damage done;
   - award of a more appropriate (or equitable) remedy such as injunction to prevent repetition of the harm being perpetrated;
   - fault, used as the reason for justifying the remedy awarded by the court;
   - punishment in the form of retributive justice;
   - deterrence;
   - economic efficiency, sometimes known as market deterrence;
   - loss distribution, or the process of spreading the losses suffered in a way that is socially acceptable;
   - insurance.
3. If the basis of dealing with tort is considered primarily from the economic viewpoint, the major choices are between the last three.
4. The law may operate by forcing manufacturers of goods to bear the cost of any harm done by defective products, in which case the consequences include:
   - passing on the cost to consumers;
   - minimising the risk by maximising safety whilst trying to achieve the most competitive price in the market place;
   - 'market deterrence' is thus obtained by reducing the overall harm that society might otherwise have suffered.

5. Alternatively, tort law can and often does operate on the basis of an individual having to bring his own claim when loss has been suffered, which means:
   - he has to prove his claim to the satisfaction of tort law in every case;
   - lack of finance or knowledge or sufficient evidence may lead to no remedy being available;
   - in other cases a third party might be obliged by law to bear the loss, e.g.:
     - vicarious liability;
     - strict liability;
     - compulsory third party motor insurance.

6. 'Loss distribution' in these ways may cause problems, e.g.:
   - fault may be ignored;
   - it may be laid at someone else's door;
   - injustice occurs when people who are good risks subsidise or compensate those who are poor risks.

7. Economic analysis of law is thus the process of theorising about such alternatives and possibilities, and Posner would say that this is the way the law in reality operates and that it is right that it should do so.

INDEX